To Nick. Th[...] [...]ly
se[r]ving our c[omm...]
President. I'm honored to have
you on the Publix Team!

Semper Fi!   MD[?]   Isa 40:31
6/25/2015

FALLING INTO GRACE

A True Story of Marines, Sabotage,
and Redemption

Michael Dietrich

Falling Into Grace
A True Story of Marines, Sabotage, and Redemption
by Michael Dietrich

Printed in the United States of America

ISBN 9781498423502

www.xulonpress.com

ENDORSEMENTS

"*NCIS* Fans Will Love *Falling Into Grace*. The amazing true story of Michael Dietrich, a United States Marine who nearly plummeted to his death when his parachute was sabotaged by a fellow Marine and then, through an odd quirk in the military legal system, was changed from the victim to the accused. The narrative is so powerful it was evidently used as the basis for the first regularly formatted show of No. 1 TV dramatic series *NCIS*."

– David Heeren
Author of thirteen books, including
What the Bible Has to Say About the USA

"A thrilling account of a terrifying ordeal utilizing terrific writing skills by a tenacious young author. I highly recommend this true story by Michael Dietrich, as he relives this perilous episode in his life. I read it in one sitting and couldn't put it down."

– Dr. Anthony Ponceti, Th.D.
Graphic Design Contributor, *Experiencing God* by Henry
and Richard Blackaby and Claude King

"A gripping true story of sabotage, survival, and salvation. Michael Dietrich gives a compelling testimony of the events surrounding his harrowing experience. Most enthralling is how Dietrich unveils God's plan of redemption."

– Major F. Damon Friedman, USAF
President, Shield of Faith Missions

"Michael Dietrich recounts his life as a young Marine leader but more importantly accounts his personal trials and tribulations of maintaining his relationship with the Almighty Leader...the Lord (I Corinthians 10:13). Dietrich's reflection of being a Marine officer and the impacts of such a life on family, are true and even more challenging when one has no Faith. Outstanding read – I didn't want to put it down!"

– Colonel Richard J. Smith, USMC (Ret)

"This true life account of the horrific event Dietrich and his Marines experienced and overcame by God's grace serves as a reminder to me that our primary focus should not be on life's circumstances, but rather on how we respond to the inevitable trials of life. Dietrich's story has encouraged me to focus more clearly on God and to be ever thankful for the peace He extends when I trust in Him...I am confident *Falling Into Grace* will encourage and inspire you as well."

– Master Chief Michelle R. Jennejahn, USN (Ret)

"*Falling Into Grace* is more than an action packed book about an accident that almost cost Dietrich his life. It is about God's unfailing love reaching out to a young man who went from simply professing to be a Christian to allowing God to transform his life. You will be gripped by this heartfelt story and challenged to reflect on your relationship with Christ. This is a must read book."

– Dr. Ron Burks
Senior Pastor, First Baptist Church Bartow
Adjunct Professor, New Orleans Baptist Theological Seminary

"If you were ever in the military and/or fell away from our Lord and Savior Jesus Christ, you will *feel* this book and know that it's totally written from the heart! The experiences that Dietrich went through in his personal life while serving on active duty will ring in you as they have in me. Knowing Dietrich personally, I know that when he came back to the Lord he was permanently changed, and it shows every day of his life."

– Clifford C. Truman, USMC 1976-1980

Direct descendant of Harry S. Truman, 33rd U.S. President

ACKNOWLEDGMENTS

Thanks to...

o My gorgeous wife, Mary. Your support and loving encouragement gave me the energy to persevere when I felt like quitting, more than once! Thank you for giving me the title of the book. I would not have been able to accomplish this project without you. I love you with all my heart.

o Harvey for being a mentor and a good friend and for sending that email about my story to our now mutual friend, David, which got this whole thing started.

o My brother, Daniel, for your encouragement and having the supernatural ability to always see the best in everyone.

o Bruce for reviewing both the initial and revised versions and for providing valuable input. You encouraged me to "prepare the field for rain" and to keep faith – thank you.

o Trish for reviewing the manuscript in the midst of the busiest month of your life – thank you.

o Ron and Jamie for your prayerful support and for always being there for me and my family.

CONTENTS

Endorsements v
Acknowledgments ix
Foreword... xiii
From the Author xv
1. Time Stood Still... 1
2. Something Sinister 4
3. Three in the Morning.. 9
4. Looking into Their Faces.. 15
5. Total Malfunction 20
6. Weakness Leaving the Body 26
7. Reliving the Terror 33
8. My Familiar Friend.. 39
9. A Hair and a Palm Print 45
10. An Enemy Within Our Ranks 53
11. A Glimpse of Cohesion 57
12. What a Marine Is Made Of 64
13. 3, 4, 6, 9: Get in Line 69
14. Where's That Stinkin' Green Light? 77
15. The Whole Truth and Nothing But 80
16. Pre-trial Confinement 85
17. Seven Thousand Miles.. 91
18. Nose to Nose 96
19. Hurricane in the Desert 101
20. Bunker! Bunker! Bunker! 109
21. Shots Fired from the Rear! 114
22. JAG 124
23. Relieved of Command 129

24. A Wrestling Match 136
25. Heart of Gold 144
26. Big on Trust 149
27. Unbecoming an Officer 155
28. Guilty? 160
29. Re-wired 163
How to Invite Jesus into Your Life 175
Endnotes 177

FOREWORD

I am blessed, honored, and proud to be able to say that I am the author's identical twin brother. Dietrich and I were the only siblings in the family growing up and were extremely close. I'd have to say that even now, I know him better than anyone else on this earth. Whenever people ask me about my brother, Dietrich, I usually tell them, "He's my hero." The reason I am so proud of Dietrich and admire him so deeply is because of his character and his infectious love for the Lord. Because he lives in Florida and I live in North Carolina, we don't get to see one another very often—usually once a year or so. I truly relish these infrequent times we are able to spend with one another and always feel "sharpened" after visiting with him and his family: "As iron sharpens iron, so one man sharpens the countenance of his friend" (Proverbs 27:17 NKJV) sums up really well how I feel after spending time with my hero...my brother, Dietrich.

Have you ever been discouraged? Or, perhaps you have been falsely accused of something? Have you been in a "no-win" situation where all possible decisions seemed to be losing propositions? Maybe you are experiencing the negative consequences of unwise choices? I would have to answer "yes" to all of these questions, and if you are like me in that regard, I implore you to read the book you are holding in your hands. Please read at least the first chapter and then decide whether or not you should continue reading on. I'm confident, after reading the first chapter, it will leave you as it did me—totally captivated! I believe with all of my heart that you are not reading this book by accident.

If I had to sum up this book in three words they would be "God's unfailing love." Psalm 13:5-6 says "I trust in Your unfailing love. My heart rejoices in Your salvation. I will sing to the LORD, for He has been good to me." My brother's transparency in vividly describing his near-death experience when participating in a military training exercise will grip your attention. The action-packed, heart-wrenching events that followed that horrible experience will stir your spirit. God's faithfulness and "working all things according to the council of His will" will inspire you to trust in Abba Father.

As I mentioned earlier, I know my brother better than anyone else I know. I can say with complete confidence that Dietrich's motivation in writing this book is to share his story to comfort a "brother or sister in need." If all of the time and sacrifice Dietrich invested into this project, which spans several years, results in helping one person to fix their eyes on Jesus in the midst of difficult circumstances, then my brother would say "mission accomplished" and "to God be the glory."

Buckle up, friend. You are about to take the ride of your life in the pages that follow. Happy reading....

–Daniel Dietrich
Captain, United States Marine Corps

FROM THE AUTHOR

This book was written for anyone who has ever been in the pit of despair with no way to dig out. For someone who wanted to wake up from the nightmare of life, only to find out that waking up was worse than the awfulness of the dream. If that describes your life right now, or if you have ever felt that way, I believe this story will encourage you. When I was in my own pit of despair, I was so beaten down by the nightmare I was facing that I could not see any way out. But in the midst of events that threatened my life and my career, God came and made Himself known to me, amazing me with the personal nature of His love. When I was at my weakest point, He showed me His magnificent strength and power. And so it is clear to me that God is the One Who pulled me up out of that pit; all the credit for the rescue goes to Him. It is my hope that, as you read my story, you will see that He is waiting to show Himself strong in your life as well.

What you're about to read is a true account of the most action-packed twelve months of my life, starting with a near-death experience in 2002. I've made every attempt to record what happened as accurately as I remember it, but my recollection of certain events may be different from the recollection of people who were involved. I've changed nearly all of the names in an effort to protect the identity and privacy of the people involved. It should also be noted that all views expressed in this work are solely mine and do not necessarily represent the position or endorsement of the United Sates Marine Corps, Navy or any other governmental agency or department, military or otherwise.

As you read about the experiences that permanently changed my heart and life, I hope you come away with a sense of awe and wonder of God's amazing love for you and me.

– Michael Dietrich

CHAPTER ONE

Time Stood Still

Every man must do two things alone; he must do his own believing and his own dying. – Martin Luther

0800 - 21 SEPTEMBER 2002   CAMP LEJEUNE, NORTH CAROLINA

Twenty Marines, seasoned jumpers, walked out on the runway to board an Air Force C-17 for a twenty-minute flight to the drop zone. The skies were clear that Saturday morning and the temperature, typical for North Carolina weather, was already in the low 80's.

Normally on liberty for the weekend, the Marines weren't as keyed up as usual over this jump. Even the men still working toward getting their gold jump wings had already made this basic daytime jump from a fixed-wing aircraft. Once we all suited up with our parachutes, though, the atmosphere changed slightly. We all loved to jump, and the Air Force C-17 is the Cadillac of military aircraft. It had all of the bells and whistles of a well-designed cargo plane, but its jet speed caused a greater shock when the parachute deployed than the force produced by the slower propeller-driven C-130.

I was slated to jump with the first stick, a group of five jumpers that would exit the aircraft in procession, one immediately after the other. For this jump, we would be exiting out of the starboard (right) side door of the aircraft from an altitude of 1,250 feet. When we were five minutes out from the drop zone (DZ), the primary jumpmaster barked out his commands over the roaring of the jet engines, with matching hand and arm signals:

1

First stick, stand up!
Hook up!
Check static lines!
Check equipment!
Sound off for equipment check!
One minute!
Thirty seconds!

Even after 28 jumps, I still got butterflies when I heard the primary jumpmaster say, "Thirty seconds!"-- knowing that in less than a minute I would be in the air, and I expected to be landing safely on the ground about three minutes later. The sensation reminded me of the feelings I had when I was dating the woman who would later become my wife: nervous and excited all at the same time.

When the light turned green, Primary Jumpmaster Herrera finally shouted, "GO!" The five of us filed out one by one and prepared to "put our knees in the breeze" while the other fifteen jumpers remained seated, waiting for their turn on a subsequent pass over the DZ. We stood in single file, arm's length apart, against the inside skin of the jet. I was the last of the first stick.

As I jumped out of the aircraft, my actions were automated and instinctive. From day one in airborne training, the steps had been drilled into me. I put my chin on my chest and my hands on the ends of the reserve chute packed in front on my waist. I put my feet and knees together, and counted out loud: "One thousand, two thousand, three thousand, four thousand. . ."

At two or three thousand, I braced myself for the customary stiff tug on my harness, signaling the fast upward pull of my parachute canopy catching air and blossoming nice and round, slowing my descent.

But something was wrong. I got to four thousand with no tug on the harness. My mind screamed, *What's going on?* This had never happened before in my previous 28 jumps. But even though I didn't know the cause of the problem, I knew what it meant: no tug on the harness meant something was critically, dangerously wrong. I looked up, over my head, and saw something I will never forget as long as I live: no parachute. Nothing. No canopy, no blossoming, nothing but the clear and empty sky. The thirty suspension lines that should have been connected to the billowing canopy of my parachute were cut away, disconnected, flapping uselessly in the wind.

Time stood still. In those few seconds, I had become trapped in every jumper's worst nightmare. Perspiration broke out on my forehead, but my mouth was dry. I kept falling, falling, staring at the frayed olive-drab lines thrashing oddly against the backdrop of a serene blue sky. The image of those frenzied lines beating the air over my head is laser-etched into my memory.

Automatically, I reached for the ripcord grip handle on my reserve parachute at the right side of my waist. Although we had been through countless training drills designed for just this scenario, I never thought it would happen to me. I pulled the T-shaped handle, expecting the reserve chute to deploy, but the handle would not budge. I looked down at it, my throat tightening, and pulled harder. It was stuck! I could not get it to come free, and my time was running out. The earth was racing up to meet me at 120 miles per hour, and I had five seconds before I was going to die.

Chapter Two

Something Sinister

All our falls are useful if they strip us of a disastrous confidence in ourselves.
– François Fénelon

A s I raced toward earth at 120 miles per hour, with no more than five seconds left to live, I pulled on the ripcord grip handle on my reserve parachute again, with all my might. I knew my life depended on this reserve chute, and I knew the seconds were quickly evaporating. This time, to my astonishment, the ripcord grip handle miraculously dislodged itself, and my reserve chute began to deploy at a 45-degree angle in front of me.

When my reserve finally caught air, I felt a sudden jolt accompanied with intense pain beyond anything I had ever experienced, as though my body had been harshly folded in half backwards. With no canopy, my descent rate had been about 120 miles per hour; when the reserve opened, the rate dropped instantly to 15 miles per hour. The intense upward force jerked my body like a ragdoll, and my lower back screamed in pain from the jolt of the reserve chute's deployment. The pain was so severe I found myself wondering whether I had broken my back. But despite the physical agony of that jolt and the wrenching grip of the pain, I was elated: at the very last second, just as the earth rose up to meet me, the parachute had opened, and life was not over for me on that warm September day.

I hit the ground two seconds later.

On the ground, I stood up cautiously, conscious of the severe hit to my back. Somehow, though, it was not broken. I slowly checked myself for injuries, took off my harness, and gathered up my reserve parachute. Death had just come ruthlessly close, and I was keenly aware of it. Two seconds away from being a fatality; much closer than I had ever planned to be, and much closer than I had ever been before. As I collected my gear and my thoughts, I realized that, incredibly, no other bones were broken, either. I had survived the jump with no main canopy and a resistant reserve chute. But then my thoughts were drawn to the jump itself: what had gone wrong with my chute? What could possibly account for these severed suspension lines? And then, another chilling thought: Did this happen to anyone else?

My mind was whirling.

Trying to speculate on what had gone wrong, I stretched out the suspension lines of my main parachute on the limp, withered North Carolina grass. Where the nylon canopy should have been attached, there were only the frayed endings of the empty lines, about four feet long. Each one of the thirty lines, which should have connected to the nylon parachute, led to nowhere. To my astonishment, there was no canopy! How could this have happened? With all these unknowns swirling in my head, I picked up my gear and double-timed it to the rally point a half-mile away on the far end of the Drop Zone. My adrenaline meter was pegged.

Drop Zone Pheasant spanned a hundred acres 20 miles southwest of Camp Lejeune and included an old airstrip used for small planes. Although the surrounding area was heavily wooded, the DZ itself had been cleared of trees and was a perfect place for our airborne operations. As I caught up with the other four jumpers at the rally point, Sergeant Mendez immediately questioned me.

"Are you all right, sir?"

Mendez, a quiet man, held the ground crew position equivalent to the jumpmaster on the aircraft. Just as Herrera supervised the jumpers in the C-17, Mendez managed the DZ crew and procedures. From the airstrip, he had watched my jump in shock, seeing my parachute fail. His eyes were locked on me as I plummeted toward the ground, wondering whether my reserve chute would ever deploy. At that moment, I had no way of knowing that two other jumpers had experienced the same problem with their main parachutes. The difference was that their reserves deployed right away, and Mendez had been flooded with relief. But he watched me continue falling with no reserve deploying, and he felt sure I was going to die. Some time later, Mendez told me that for weeks after the jump he would wake up with nightmares about the incident, watching me fall to my death in the dream. At the site that day, though, I couldn't tell how shaken up this quiet, reserved Marine really was. He had just watched his lieutenant nearly die on a routine training mission.

Mendez repeated the question: "Sir, are you all right?"

"Yeah. I...I'm fine," I nodded slowly, amazed that it was true: no broken back, and not even a sprained ankle. Somehow, the adrenalin rush was overriding any pain caused by the severe jolt, but only temporarily, as I was to discover: the next morning I would be unable to bend over and put on my boots.

"They're on the way back to Cherry Point, sir. The rest of the operation is cancelled," he told me, his expression grave. As head of the DZ crew, Mendez was in contact with the pilot after every pass, making sure things were proceeding as planned. But when he saw the reserve chutes deploying, he knew something was horribly wrong, and immediately called the pilot to cancel the mission.

Just then Puller and Valez, two of the other four jumpers in my stick, walked up to me and said, "Did you have to pull your reserve, too?"

I stared at them, not sure I had heard Puller correctly. Did he just tell me they had to pull their reserves as well?

A few feet away, Puller and Valez had stretched out their harnesses and suspension lines side by side on the old concrete runway. Following suit, I removed my harness from the aviator's kit bag and laid it out beside theirs, and the three of us scanned the gear: three identical damaged parachutes with three sets of suspension lines cut away in the same manner. From the basic harness, 15 lines of olive-drab 550-cord stretched out from each shoulder strap, attached on both shoulders to a silver buckle fastener. From each of those lines, 7 white nylon inner cords splayed out of their olive drab casings, further accenting the damage. The parachutes looked like three empty packages, ruined by the sheared-off lines. It was grim. The gear reminded me of bodies with missing limbs; they should never look like this, and they should never be seen like this. I knew what the other two men were thinking: the day could have ended much differently for the three of us. Veteran jumpers as we were, we were chilled by the sight.

"Look at that, Puller," I said, pointing to the severed lines. "They're the same. The lines are all cut at the same length. *The same length.* What do you think it means?"

By this time, some of the ground crew had walked up behind us. Everyone stared at the ruined chutes stretched out on the concrete. No one had ever seen anything like it, and we were taken aback at the sight of the butchered equipment. After a few minutes, someone in the group came up with a possible explanation: "Could there have been a sharp edge on the door? When you jumped, the sharp edge would have cut the lines."

We all considered this possibility, looking down on the tattered chutes lying on the pavement. Could a jagged edge on the door have done this? Was something rough or serrated enough to cut all those lines? Something about it didn't ring true, though. Before every jump, the jumpmaster runs his hand along the hatch opening to check for any rough edge that might hang up the jumper, much less a sharp, jagged piece of metal that could potentially cut suspension lines. We trusted him to do a careful evaluation of the hatch. *Well, it's possible,* I thought; *not likely, but possible.* That could be the answer. The suggestion, improbable as it was, seemed to make more sense than anything else. Puller and Valez nodded.

Lance Corporal Rayvens, part of the DZ crew, stepped closer and repeated the idea he had just put forward. "Yeah, that must have been what caused the problem. There must have been a sharp edge on the door. Look," he said, gesturing toward the damaged gear on the asphalt. "They're all cut at the same spot!"

Back in the aircraft with the rest of the jumpers, Herrera had realized there had been some kind of critical failure. After I exited the aircraft, he began to retrieve the static lines and deployment bags as he normally would. As he pulled the static lines and deployment bags dragging alongside the airplane back into the aircraft, Herrera got the shock of his life. Three of the five deployment bags still had the parachutes inside! They should have been empty. Those parachutes should have been connected to the suspension lines, blossoming out to slow the descents of the jumpers. One of those canopies belonged to me, and the other two belonged to Corporal Valez and Chief Warrant Officer Puller. Finding a deployment bag with a parachute still inside after a jump had never happened before, and Herrera was stunned.

By this time, the C-17 with Herrera and the remaining fifteen jumpers had flown back to the airfield in Cherry Point. While we were standing on the asphalt mystified by the frayed lines of our lifeless chutes, the duty cell phone rang at the DZ. Mendez handed me the phone. "Sir, it's Sergeant Herrera. He wants to talk to you."

"Is everyone okay, sir?" Herrera asked. As jumpmaster, he had the unenviable job of watching me exit the aircraft and struggle to deploy my reserve chute. Since Herrera was running the operation, he felt his responsibility deeply, and his voice was shaking.

"We're all fine, sergeant," I told him. "Puller, Valez, and I had to pull our reserves. The only thing we can come up with is that there must have been a sharp edge on the door, because the lines were all cut to the same length."

He hesitated, and then replied tensely, "Sir, when we got back, I took off my own parachute and opened it up. All the suspension lines were cut."

"What are you talking about, Sergeant Herrera?" I asked. My head was spinning, but I stood there motionless. He was no longer making sense. "The suspension lines on *your* chute were cut? You didn't even jump, sergeant. How could your lines be cut?"

He paused. "Sir, something told me to open up my parachute. I'm telling you, when I unpacked it, I could see that all of my lines were cut."

I was astonished. *That makes four of us*, I thought: Puller, Valez, Herrera, and me. Something else was going on here. Apparently there was no sharp edge on the hatch, no jagged metal ripping the lines, because Herrera's lines were cut even though he didn't jump. And even if there had been a sharp serrated edge on the hatch, the jumpmaster would have detected it in his routine check of the opening before we jumped. Now I knew clearly that there was no oversight we could point to and account for this. There was no easy explanation for the severed lines. Instead, a sense of something sinister, something dirty, something malicious was beginning to show its face.

Herrera went on, his voice tight with anger. "Sir, someone cut the lines on purpose. This is a criminal act."

For the second time that day, time stood still. As I tried to process what he had just said, my sense of hearing vanished. I heard the sound of Herrera's voice, but I could not believe the words he said. Those five words-- *This is a criminal act*-- would change my life and turn my world upside down.

CHAPTER THREE

Three in the Morning

Do not fear the conflict, and do not flee from it; where there is no struggle, there is no virtue. – John of Kronstadt

DZ PHEASANT ,
1015 - 21 SEPTEMBER 2002   CAMP LEJEUNE, NORTH CAROLINA

This is a criminal act.

Those words from Sergeant Herrera echoed through my mind. I hung up the phone at the Drop Zone and stared at the ground; everything was numb. The idea that my parachute lines could have been cut intentionally had not occurred to me until now. Sabotage, a very foul word, hadn't even crossed my mind.

Suddenly, a torrent of thoughts and questions came rushing through me. *Who would do such a thing? Was it someone in the platoon? Why would a fellow Marine do this?* Whoever did this was hanging his hopes on getting away with it free and clear. I wanted, at that moment, to find him and bring him to justice. This idea of planning intentional destruction with equipment designed to save the lives of Marines jumping from aircraft was so foreign to me, so repulsive. I could have been killed. Puller and Valez could have been killed. And how many other Marines? I was chilled by the thought of such an evil, deadly idea. These questions, among many others, would result in an ongoing investigation that would last over a year.

The DZ crew gathered our gear and drove back to Camp Lejeune while I drove to the airfield to link up with Herrera. By the time that I got to the airfield, Criminal Investigation Division (CID), the Marine counterpart of the

9

Naval Criminal Investigative Service (NCIS), was already there. They were combing the C-17 that I had jumped from just a few hours before, looking for evidence and dusting for fingerprints. Herrera and I stood together on the tarmac, watching the team entering and exiting the aircraft and conferring with each other over their notes. Herrera was extremely upset about the sinister spirit of the morning's events, and kept saying over and over, "I can't believe this, sir – a rigger *in our own platoon* tried to kill us!" He knew that all of us packed the parachutes, and no one outside our platoon had access to the paraloft, where we packed and stored the chutes. Herrera was convinced it was an inside job.

Sabotage, of course, is nothing new. Exactly how old it is may not be clear. During the Civil War, for example, Union troops destroyed train rails by creating what were called Sherman's Neckties. The Yanks made a bonfire of the railroad ties and put the rails on the fire. When the rails were hot enough to bend, they twisted them so the rails could not be reused, thus ending Confederate deliveries.[1] And back in 1942, the Nazis set down men off Long Island and the coast of Florida with a mission of destroying trains, power plants, canals, and factories.[2] Sabotage affects the world with its malicious desire to wipe out critical resources; but in most cases, damage is done to the equipment belonging to a foreign enemy, not to the equipment of those in your own unit. Even "friendly fire," as tragic and fatal as that can be, wounds through grievous error; sabotage, though, is intentional. The idea of having a saboteur in our own platoon was repulsive.

For their probe into this sabotage event, CID took possession of all twenty parachutes: the five that I brought with me from the DZ, three of which had cut lines; the chute that Herrera took off his back; and the fourteen unopened chutes from the jumpers who did not jump after the remaining passes over the DZ were cancelled.

That evening, at nearby Camp Johnson, I met up with CID and now NCIS, who had joined the effort and would soon take over the investigation. By the time I got there, it was nearly midnight, and my energy was fading fast. When I walked into the room where they had secured the parachutes, and saw all twenty lying on the floor, the sight of those butchered chutes was chilling. I was still reeling from my all-too-personal encounter with death, and still trying to come up with some type of motive.

One of the NCIS investigators said, "Those five parachutes over there are the ones from the Drop Zone. Three of them had cut lines, and one was yours. That one right there is the one that Herrera had on that had cut lines as well. All of those," he continued, pointing to the far side of the room, "are the fourteen that weren't jumped."

I quickly noticed that all fourteen of those chutes had been popped open, but I couldn't tell what condition they were in from where I was standing.

Guessing what I was wondering about, the investigator proceeded with his findings. "We opened up all of those, and nine of those fourteen had cut suspension lines. All thirteen of the chutes that were cut were done in the exact same spot and in the same way."

My stomach was churning; I thought I was going to throw up. Watching one of our jumpers die would have been tragic; finding out someone from our platoon deliberately caused it would have been unbearable. But now, I was looking at a planned execution: those thirteen ruined chutes could have meant thirteen dead Marines. Even having a reserve chute didn't take away the grisly sight of those severed lines, because statistically the malfunction rate of reserves is 50%. The math nerd in me calculated that the probability of all three of our reserve chutes opening when needed was only 12.5%. Statistically speaking, at least one of the three of us should have died on that drop zone.

"How many more parachutes are there?" the investigators asked me.

"We've got about a hundred chutes total but only twenty of those with white, twenty-foot static lines like these for C-17 jumps," I explained.

One of the questions burning through everyone's mind was impossible to ignore: *Why cut only thirteen chutes and not all twenty?* There were so many unknowns. But one thing had unfortunately become clear after seeing the expert way the chutes were cut and then re-packed. Whoever did this was a parachute rigger who knew exactly what he was doing. To cut the lines, someone would have had to take the parachute out of the pack tray and cut all 30 suspension lines on the outside of the deployment bag with heavy-duty rigger shears. Then he would have to re-pack the parachute and deployment bag back inside the pack tray in such a way that the jumper who was randomly assigned the chute wouldn't notice anything wrong, and the jumpmaster conducting an inspection of that parachute after the jumper was suited up wouldn't notice anything, either. This was painstakingly and maliciously done.

I headed back on base to meet with the Battalion Commanding Officer (CO), Battalion Executive Officer (XO), and the Battalion Sergeant Major

(SgtMaj). The XO and the SgtMaj had both earned their gold wings several years previously while serving in other units, so they had the background to understand the critical details of the incident.

It was now about two in the morning on Sunday, 22 September 2002, as I walked slowly up to the single-story Battalion Headquarters building to meet them. We met outside in the glare of a single light pole. I rendered a salute to the CO and XO and said, "Good morning, gentlemen."

The Commanding Officer reached out and shook my hand as he said, "I'm glad we still have you with us, Lieutenant Dietrich."

"Me, too, sir."

The Executive Officer and fellow gold winger looked at me in disbelief. "So you had to pull your reserve?"

"Yes, sir."

He frowned, trying to get some perspective on the incident. "What happened with your reserve?"

I explained how my first two attempts to pull my reserve were unsuccessful and that finally on the third pull, my ripcord handle came loose.

The XO processed that information. "How long did you have after your reserve deployed before you hit the ground?"

I looked at him, swallowed, and said, "Not long, sir. 'One thousand, two thousand'. . . I was on the ground."

He shook his head in wonder. He hadn't jumped in years, and he might have been considering the consequences if he had been jumping that day using the parachute I was assigned.

"Go home, Lieutenant," the CO said. "Get some sleep and we'll sort through all of this on Monday." Standing there outside headquarters in the middle of the night, none of us expected the onslaught of media attention and press that would hit us in the days to come.

It was three in the morning when I finally got home. I had jumped from an aircraft with a defective parachute, with an almost-defective reserve chute, and most likely with a fellow jumper who had cut my suspension lines. I had been through the most frightening event of my life, I had been awake for nearly twenty-four hours straight, and I was totally exhausted, both physically and emotionally. When I walked in the front door of our small brick house, I found my wife Mary in the darkened living room, sitting on the old sleeper sofa my grandparents had given me. We didn't have much other furniture and our words echoed off the hardwood floors as we talked.

Mary rushed over to me, concerned at the unusually late hour. "I thought you'd never get home! Is everything okay, Dietrich?"

I took a deep breath and exhaled. "Nope."

"What's wrong?" she asked, her eyes clouded with worry. "What happened? Why are you so late getting home?"

"I don't want to talk about it." For some reason, the weight of the events was too heavy for me to put my reactions into words. I was so exhausted, so spent, that describing it one more time was too much.

Mary knew something was terribly wrong. She put her arms around me and held me tight, and I felt the soft swelling of her pregnancy press against me. The realization that I almost died hit me full force: my death today would have made her a widow who was pregnant with my child. Our son, our daughter, and the new baby would have had no father. My children would have grown up without me. The impact of all that abruptly crashed down on me, and I began crying and shuddering from the strain of the day. Mary's worry turned into alarm: she had never seen me break down.

"Dietrich," she pleaded, "tell me what happened on the jump!"

"I almost died," I gasped. "Someone cut the lines on my parachute."

"They did *what*?! Who would do such a thing?" Mary's eyes grew wide with disbelief. She knew the level of trust we had in our platoon. She knew we never checked to see who packed our chutes because we all had complete faith in each other. She asked question after question, frowning first with astonishment and then with growing anger, as the events of the day came into sharper focus to her. Finally, her questions ran out and she sat back against the sofa, overwhelmed to think I had almost died on a routine jump.

Both of us were exhausted and needed some rest. I was drained from the jump, the tension, and the disturbing questions about the parachutes. Finally, I fell into an uneasy sleep.

Sunday morning, I woke up sore. Every muscle in my body resisted movement. My lower back was in extreme pain, especially on the left side. That night, I got ready to put Thomas, who was three, and Larissa, our eighteen-month-old, in the tub, as I did every night after work. But I couldn't lift my children in and out of the bathtub. I tried, but I couldn't; the pain was excruciating. Even putting on my shoes was agony. I tried to bend over to put them on, but I couldn't lace them and tie them to save my life. For over two weeks, Mary had to help me put on my socks and my boots because the pain stabbed me like a knife when I tried bending over. And every time I saw my pregnant wife lean over to help me put on my boots, I grew outraged all over again at the person responsible for putting me in that condition. It was hard to think about anything else.

CHAPTER FOUR

Looking into Their Faces

Revenge [...] is like a rolling stone, which, when a man hath forced up a hill, will return upon him with a greater violence. – Albert Schweitzer

23 SEPTEMBER 2002   CAMP LEJEUNE, NORTH CAROLINA

On Monday morning, I arrived at the paraloft hoping the investigation would be completed quickly so we could get back to preparing for deployment. By 13 December, our platoon had to prepare and inventory our gear, complete embarkation forms, and dedicate all of our air delivery equipment (six million dollars worth of cargo parachutes, personnel parachutes, and cargo drop rigging equipment) to a specific shipping container to be loaded at the port in Morehead City for shipment to Kuwait. As critical as our deployment tasks were, though, I soon realized we would have to handle them against the backdrop of the investigation, which would be an enormous distraction. I began to understand that things would never be the same for me and my platoon.

Being a part of Air Delivery Platoon and earning my jump wings was rooted deep in the imagination of my childhood. Ever since I can remember, even as early as six years old, I have wanted to parachute out of an airplane. The idea of jumping from a plane and floating to the ground with my parachute above me catching the wind fascinated me, and I thought about it all the time. And so, with the creativity programmed into children everywhere, I came up with my own version: homemade parachutes. First, I would cut an old pillowcase into squares and make holes in each one of the corners. Then I would use some of my mom's sewing thread to convert it into a parachute, and attach one of my army men. Decked out in my own cape, which was

15

a long bath towel tied around my neck, I'd climb into the tree in our back yard, hang on to a branch with one arm, and fling the army man up in the air as high as I could. Then I would jump out of the tree and catch it before it hit the ground.

I played this parachute game for hours on end, never tiring of catching my army man in his chute, dreaming that one day I would be the man floating to the ground. The game never lost its appeal, and many years later, lo and behold, I ended up getting a job where I was paid to do the very same thing. I even earned a little extra for my parachute jumps; in 2002, jump pay was an additional $150 per month. Jumping out of an aircraft with a parachute was one of the things I enjoyed most about my job. A little boy's dream come true, until the events of 21 September 2002, when the investigation got underway and the appeal began to fade.

The distraction of the investigation, just as I feared, was great. The men were understandably nervous about the implications of the sabotage, and their uneasiness displayed itself in some unexpected ways. For example, some of my Marines were not even on base. My platoon sergeant informed me that several Marines had booked hotel rooms in Jacksonville over the weekend because they didn't want to sleep in the barracks. After thinking over the details of the jump and picturing the severed lines of the chutes, they had come to the conclusion that it was an inside job, and paranoia was running wild. Even though I could understand their concern, I was disturbed that they could not bring themselves to sleep in the barracks on base; their reluctance to do so demonstrated a grave loss of trust, one I should have known was coming. I hated it. Had the person who cut the lines foreseen this consequence of his crime?

We were training hard, getting ready to deploy into combat together to fight the enemy, to engage in the war on terrorism. Part of this readiness included honing our skills in rigging equipment such as our High Mobility Multipurpose Wheeled Vehicles (HMMWVs) for airdrop. These four-wheel-drive armored powerhouses with strengthened suspension systems required three 100-foot diameter cargo parachutes. For training, we had an old one without an engine that we used to practice rigging. In addition, we were also rigging smaller items such as ammunition and MREs (meals ready to eat). We were PTing (physical training) a lot as well, and I really enjoyed taking the platoon out on formation runs. After all we had been through, these runs were relaxing, even though I was forced to reduce our running time to allow for the hours expended in the investigation. My back remained sore from the jump incident, but I loved the runs we made: about seven miles through a wooded trail behind the paraloft.

As we went through preparations to deploy, though, the foundation of confidence in each other, especially as parachute riggers, was eroding. The idea that the enemy was in our midst was never very far from our thoughts, and it was the uninvited guest in every hour of the day.

The parachute operation that turned my world upside down took place in September of 2002, a little more than a year after the catastrophic events of September 2001. It would be my twenty-ninth parachute jump. I had been the Air Delivery Platoon Commander for about a year and a half, and I knew my job and my Marines extremely well . . . or so I thought.

One of the unique attributes of a parachute rigger platoon is the close bond that develops among the Marines. In general, Marines are a band of brothers. Even now, after being a civilian for many years, I consider myself a Marine. According to the 35th Commandant of the Marine Corps, General James F. Amos, it's a lifetime connection. "You're a Marine, just in a different uniform and you're in a different phase of your life. But you'll always be a Marine because you went to Parris Island, San Diego or the hills of Quantico. There's no such thing as a former Marine."

With a parachute rigger platoon, though, that bond goes even deeper than the comrades-at-arms connection of other Marines. Every day, we placed our lives in each others' hands, trusting that every rigger packed every chute correctly. People tend to think that each jumper packs his own chute, and although that was true with the Paramarines in World War II, that is not the case now. Chutes are packed by riggers, men who have been trained to pack them. Very few parachute jumpers attend the intensive schooling required to pack the parachutes as well, but every man in our platoon had also trained to rig the parachutes. Our platoon was one of only three in the entire Marine Corps in which all jumpers were also riggers. The safety and survival of every jumper depended on the focused, intentional care used by the riggers on each chute. Without question, we trusted each other. If, for example, the parachute had been folded the wrong way, the expanding canopy would have friction. Friction means heat, and heat means holes in the canopy. Or if the suspension lines were twisted during packing, they could bind up or even break. In addition, should the lines become tangled so that the chute doesn't unfold correctly, the motion could violently twist the jumper or even snap his neck. To prevent these problems, one rigger watches while another packs the chute, following a specific 7-point "pack in process" inspection checklist. Even the reserve chutes, never deployed, were repacked once a year per regulation. The initials of the riggers, the pack-in-process inspectors, and the date are written in the small log record book attached to the parachute harness.

The Rigger's Pledge, in part, said:

> *I will never pass over any defect, nor neglect any repair, no matter how small, as I know that omissions and mistakes in the rigging of a parachute may cost a life.*
>
> *I will keep all parachute equipment entrusted to my care in the best possible condition, remembering always that little things left undone cause major troubles.*
>
> *I will never let the idea that a piece of work is "good enough" make me a potential murderer through a careless mistake or oversight, for I know there can be no compromise with perfection.*

For all of us in the platoon, consequently, packing the chutes correctly was second nature. The Pledge ends with the rigger motto "I will be sure - always." And in fact, never once did I have any doubts about my parachute. I never spent time wondering whether it would open correctly; I never wondered who packed it. I was as confident in the integrity of my fellow riggers as I was that the sun would rise in the East the next day. We were a fraternal brotherhood of the highest order, and I considered them family. I trusted those men with my life, and they trusted me with theirs. Always.

So when my platoon sergeant informed me that several of the Marines had booked hotel rooms, I had clear evidence that the severed lines had broken the bond of trust we had built. Not only had the men lost confidence in their fellow riggers, they were now unable to depend on their personal safety in the barracks. This hit me hard, because as the platoon commander, I was responsible for the safety and morale of my Marines. The parachute sabotage was now affecting all of us.

When I checked into this further, several men stated firmly that they would not jump again until the investigation was complete and the riggers responsible were in the brig. A few even went so far as to say that they would be court-martialed before they would jump again. They were ready to die for their country; Marines had always been ready to give their lives. What they were not willing to do, however, was to die for no reason at all: simply because someone decided to cut the lifeline of a man jumping from a plane. These Marines were seriously analyzing the incident of the previous Saturday, and they didn't like what they were seeing. This was a leadership challenge unlike any I had ever faced.

27 SEPTEMBER 2002 CAMP LEJEUNE, NORTH CAROLINA

That Friday, I got word from battalion headquarters that NCIS wanted to see the entire platoon, so I called a formation at the paraloft to explain the situation to them. The Marines were in standard formation of three ranks, and after they formed at attention I gave the command, "At ease."

"We're all going down to NCIS after formation, so the investigators can talk to us," I explained. "This is what they do, and they're good at it. While this investigation is ongoing, though, we all need to stick together. If there was ever a time that we needed to be a band of brothers, it's right now. We're a family, and we need to watch each other's back."

As I was addressing the platoon and looking into each of their faces, I couldn't help but think that one, or maybe more than one, was the source of this evil. As I talked about how our platoon was a family and how we had always trusted each other, another incident of treachery came to mind. Standing before my Marines, I thought about Judas, one of the closest friends of Jesus Christ. Judas was not just an ordinary Christ-follower, but he was one of the Twelve, one of the chosen. After spending three years on the road with Jesus, sharing supper around the campfire and listening to Jesus give His insight into the everyday struggles of life on earth, Judas identified Jesus to a band of soldiers on a trumped-up charge. As I looked into the eyes of my men, I thought about Judas, and I hate to admit that I began to question every one of them. Who was it? Who had made the choice to betray?

Chapter Five

Total Malfunction

A person's life is his most precious possession. Consequently, to rob him of it is the greatest sin we can commit against him, while to give one's own life on his behalf is the greatest possible expression of love for him. – John Stott

3 OCTOBER 2000 CAMP LEJEUNE, NORTH CAROLINA

Although my work life centered on the Eagle, Globe, and Anchor, I also had an important job as husband and father to my little family of three. In October of 2000, when Thomas was almost two years old, Mary was three months pregnant with our second child. I remember that my heart was beginning to soften slightly to spiritual things, and I could finally sense, after years of running from God, that He was inviting me back. And I did respond. I started talking to God again, and reading the Bible occasionally. I had just learned that I would be leading a platoon in Beach and Terminal Operations Company (BTO), and we were renting a nice house in town while we waited for our chance for on-base housing. The couple living next door to us at that time was Mormons; the husband was an officer in the Navy, and Mary and his wife became good friends.

At this point, Mary had not yet made the choice to ask Jesus to be the Lord of her life, and she began asking questions about what our Mormon neighbors believed. She wondered how their ideas about God were different from mine.

"One of the main differences is that they think the good things they do for God will earn them a spot in heaven," I told her. "Christians believe that getting into heaven is based on understanding that Jesus died on the cross but rose again from the grave. When you say 'yes' to Him, you depend on

20

Jesus to take away the sin barrier that keeps you from facing God. Then the good things you do are just proof that you know Him personally and you have a place in heaven, not what you do to earn a place there."

Mary listened to my answer and thought it over carefully. "Well, how do you know that you're right and they're wrong?" she asked.

I tried to give her a solid answer, but it was very much like the incoherent words of someone with limited eyesight trying to explain the stunning beauty of a rainbow. Many years had gone by since I had been "abiding in Christ," spending regular time with Him and listening to the whisper of the Holy Spirit. I could give her only a basic, theoretical answer. And Mary knew the condition of my heart. She knew better than anyone else what was important to me, and she could see I was not practicing what I was preaching. Andrew Murray refers to "abiding in Christ" as a "willing, intelligent, and whole-hearted surrender by which we accept His offer, and consent to the abiding in Him as the only life we choose." He likens it to a king, attending to the business of his army, his treaties, and every other kingly concern, yet all the while keeping his "consciousness of royalty."[3] In today's world, that means doing our jobs and going about our business, all the while knowing we belong to a heavenly kingdom. I knew my walk with Jesus couldn't be classified as "whole-hearted surrender," and being able to give only rudimentary answers to my wife's genuine questions about Him made me wish I put the same effort into following Jesus that I put into the Marine Corps.

Seeing again how inadequate my understanding was of the things of God, I decided that we should start going to church. So one Saturday, we drove around the city of Jacksonville, North Carolina, and found the First Baptist Church near downtown. Mary didn't really want to go, but I persuaded her to visit once, promising that if she didn't like it we didn't have to go back. After a long, long time, we were finally attending a church service together as a family. I had not been to church in several years by that time, and Mary had gone only as a little girl.

As we drove home that Sunday I asked Mary what she thought. "So, what was your impression? Did you like it?"

She was honest to a fault. "Not particularly," she said, "but the people were really nice, I thought."

We began to attend church there on an infrequent basis, once every month or two. Looking back now, I realize I was what the book of Revelation describes as a "lukewarm Christian," a believer who is halfhearted and indifferent. This attitude is very distasteful to God. In fact, the Bible explains in Chapter 3 of Revelation that the lukewarm Christian makes God want to throw up. W. A Criswell, Bible teacher and preacher, described this point of view in a sermon. "Why, one church is as good as another, and one doctrine is as good as another, and one theology is as good as another, and one system is as good as another. What difference does it make?" God didn't think that one God was as good as another. Hot water was useful for medicinal purposes, and cold water quickly quenched a man's thirst, but lukewarm water has neither benefit. God would prefer me either hot or cold, and my "playing church" was making Him sick.

On the home front, Mary continued to feel well as she carried our second child. Thomas was doing fine, there were no problems with her pregnancy, and we were glad everything was progressing without incident. Unfortunately, though, I did little to support her along the way. In fact, I was so worried about my reputation as the new lieutenant on campus that I told my beautiful wife I would be unable to help her as I did when Thomas was on the way. "Mary," I explained to her one night when Thomas was in bed asleep, "I'm not going to be able to go with you to all of your appointments like I did with Thomas. I have a lot of new responsibilities now and I just can't take all of that time off."

Mary was such a strong and independent person that she was able to manage things even without the support I should have been giving her. She could have complained that she felt like a single parent and that I wasn't being the husband she needed me to be. Occasionally, we did spend time together as a family; for example, we went out to eat every Saturday and we drove to Washington, D.C., one weekend. Mary enjoyed those times tremendously. And she never said anything negative about our Marine Corps life; she was very understanding. She didn't question; she didn't argue. What I didn't tell her, though, was what my commanding officer had told me: take whatever time I needed for her appointments. Somehow, I thought he didn't really mean that, and if I had taken him at his word, going with Mary to the doctor's appointments, I was afraid it would affect my record.

Even now, I'm ashamed to admit it, but I put a higher value on what my fellow officers thought of me than what my wife thought of me or what she needed from me. My urgent need to be the best and to impress my leadership with my work ethic far outweighed my inclination to take care of my wife and

our unborn baby. Pride, not concern, was driving my agenda. I was more concerned with my reputation on the base than with the emotional health of my
long-suffering wife at home. I was missing the boat in a critical way: my pride
in the status of my career was my main focus. By centering all my energies on
myself, I was missing a more meaningful relationship with my wife and with
my God. Even though we were going to church occasionally, even though I
was reading the Bible once in a while, my first priority was myself. This was a
sin of self-importance, and the Lord was patiently waiting for me to repent.

In the meantime, our second child was born, our sweet little daughter
Larissa, in March of 2001. I was now the proud father of a two-year-old boy
and a beautiful baby girl. But I wasn't being the best husband and father I
could be. Mary knew it, and God knew it, too.

21 SEPTEMBER 2002 CAMP LEJEUNE, NORTH CAROLINA

Every jump was layered in drill and practice designed to prevent injury,
and 21 September was no exception.

The day of the incident, we had all mustered that morning at the paraloft
where the platoon headquarters was located aboard Camp Lejeune, in order
to go through pre-jump training and load the parachutes to transport them
to the airfield. We conducted this training before each and every jump,
and everyone participating was required to go through it, regardless of the
number of jumps or amount of experience or rank a Marine had.

The primary jumpmaster (PJ) led all of the jumpers in safety drills.
For this parachute operation, Sergeant Herrera was the PJ. I liked Sergeant
Herrera a lot. He was from the country of Columbia and knew how to
motivate his Marines. If I observed something that I didn't like and wanted
someone to "tighten them up" a little, I would go to Herrera. He would
simply say, "I'll take care of it, sir," in his thick Columbian accent. And sure
enough, the results I wanted shortly followed.

The Marines called him a "stress monster," and I suppose he was a bit high-
strung, but he had an eye for detail and knew how things should be done. This
was a good trait when it came to being a PJ, who was the person ultimately
responsible for the lives of the jumpers in a given parachute operation.

That Saturday morning Herrera gathered us in a circle, double-arms
interval in the cargo floor packing lanes, where we had plenty of room to
spread out. Part of the pre-jump training involved rehearsing what to do in

the event of a mishap. For example, we practiced for situations like landing in the water, landing in power lines, tree landings, colliding with another jumper in mid-air, and partial and total malfunctions. For partial and total parachute malfunctions, we practiced how to deploy our reserve parachutes located on the front of our waists. It was easy to be half-hearted about the practice; a Marine with twenty years in a jump platoon would most likely never have had to pull his reserve. So none of us looked forward to going through these drills; we had performed pre-jump exercises hundreds of times in the past and knew that we would most likely never encounter any of those scenarios. But as the leader, I knew that I had to set the example, and I had to remind the troops from time to time about the importance of pre-jump safety training. I didn't want them to "half-step" the training: I wanted them to give 100%.

After we had gone through our drills, we went outside and rehearsed in-flight operations and followed the PJ's pre-jump commands. For this jump, we planned to have four "sticks" of five jumpers and make four different passes over the drop zone (DZ). A "stick" is a group of jumpers that exit the aircraft in procession, one immediately after the other. And last of all, we practiced the correct way to fall on the ground as we landed under our parachutes, also known as parachute landing falls (PLFs). This drill was not a crowd favorite, either, but it was essential for our safety.

Another important step was steering the parachute so that the jumper was facing the wind, or "holding" with the wind, and not running with the wind. I made that mistake on my first parachute jump during airborne training at Fort Benning, Georgia, and had a migraine for two days afterward as a reminder to never do that again. One of the phrases the airborne instructors used all the time to help us remember to hold with the wind was "Hold what ya got, Airborne." We also practiced steering our pretend chutes into the wind.

When we had completed all the pre-jump training, we went to the parachute locker and retrieved twenty C-17 parachutes to load into the truck to take to the airfield. C-17 jumps were unique in that we had to use special parachute rigs with a different static line. The static line is a cord that connects the aircraft and the jumper. One end is hooked to a thick, tightly-wound rope cable inside the plane, and the other hooks onto the jumper's deployment bag (D-bag), which contains his parachute. As he falls, the static line grows taut, and this tension pulls the D-bag out of the container on his back. The jumpmaster pulls the static line and the D-bag back into the plane as the jumper descends. A standard parachute had a yellow 15-foot static line attached to the deployment bag, but a C-17 parachute had a white 20-foot static line. We had over 100 parachutes in the locker but only 20 had white static lines. After we loaded our gear onto the truck and the DZ crew loaded their gear into the HMMWV, we departed the Camp Lejeune paraloft. The DZ crew led by Sergeant Mendez left for DZ Pheasant, and the rest of us headed for the air station about an hour away in Cherry Point.

Once we had unloaded the parachutes and the rest of our gear, I found the Air Force air crew and pilots and conducted some last-minute liaison with them. While I was talking with the easygoing Air Force captain who was the pilot for the mission, he told me, "You can drop the 'sir,' Dietrich. We're both officers. Just call me Jim." His casual treatment of the difference in our ranks illustrated the difference in culture between the Marine Corps and the Air Force. As a Marine first lieutenant, I would not dream of addressing a Marine Corps captain by his first name. It's simply something that you didn't do. It was, "Yes, sir" and "No, sir," plain and simple. Naturally, I didn't take this pilot up on his offer, but I really appreciated the friendliness that motivated him to mention it.

After we completed our final planning, we began to get suited up and to don our parachutes using the buddy system: one jumper got his parachute on first with the other Marine assisting him. Parachutes were randomly issued, reflecting the rigger code, "I will be sure always." Each parachute had a small log record book inside a pocket on one of the canvas straps, listing who last packed and inspected that chute. But we didn't care which parachute we got, because we trusted each and every Marine in the platoon with our lives every time we exited the aircraft with a harness on.

After suiting up, a jumpmaster was required to perform a jumpmaster parachute inspection (JMPI). The jumpmaster had to ensure that each parachutist had his rig on correctly and that there wasn't anything faulty with his equipment. In addition, he made certain there weren't any broken or frayed straps or twisted lines, he checked the static line, and he thoroughly inspected each jumper's reserve parachute.

With all the pre-jump exercises behind us, all twenty jumpers walked out on the runway and boarded the C-17. As our plane lifted off, we began the twenty-minute flight bound for the DZ, where the detachment from Air Delivery Platoon was ready to receive us. None of us ever imagined that warm Saturday morning that we were going to be jumping with 13 damaged parachutes from an aircraft 1,250 feet in the air.

CHAPTER SIX

Weakness Leaving the Body

God uses chronic pain and weakness, along with other afflictions, as his chisel for sculpting our lives. – J.I. Packer

15 JUNE 1995   FLORIDA

My interest in parachutes had been with me since childhood, but my interest in the Marine Corps came through my twin brother, Daniel. In the summer of 1995, I was taking night classes at the University of South Florida (USF) in Tampa and interning at a local bakery plant. During that time, Daniel, who had been working in a big box store, was recruited in the parking lot, went to boot camp, and came back a new man. The change was remarkable. He went to Parris Island a somewhat timid guy, but he returned as a strong and confident Marine. Daniel now had a calm self-assurance; he had been pushed to his limit and beyond to earn the title of United States Marine. The Marine Corps commercials say "The change is forever," and nine months later, I was impressed enough with my brother's new self-reliance that I decided to do the same thing.

During Daniel's training, the Orlando Officer Selection Office (OSO) gave a presentation to his reserve unit on the Marine Corps officer program, detailing a plan for college students to attend Officer Candidate School (OCS) during the summers.

"They said you can go to OCS while you're in college," Daniel told me, "and then receive a commission as a second lieutenant after you get your degree."

After hearing that, I was ready to take the plunge. It sounded intimidating and exhilarating at the same time. With Daniel's stories about the severity and harshness of boot camp and the forced march hikes running through my mind, I started training and shed the fifteen pounds I had gained interning at the bakery. I got a rope to practice climbing and a pull-up bar to do pull-ups every evening after night class.

According to the Orlando Officer Selection Officer (OSO), the program was extremely competitive and there was no guarantee that I would be accepted. They told me there were two things that would really help my "package": being an engineering major and getting a high score on the Armed Services Vocational Aptitude Battery (ASVAB).

"What you need to focus on now is getting into shape and preparing for the physical fitness test (PFT)," they told me. "The minimum score is 250, but you need to be at least 275 to be competitive."

That was not what I wanted to hear. I was light-years away; I wasn't even close to a 250. The PFT consisted of a three-mile run, sit-ups, and dead-hang pull-ups, which was the part that hurt my score most. Twenty pull-ups earned a perfect score of 100 points with a 5-point deduction for every one fewer than 20, and I could do only 7 at a time.

With that in mind, I began PT"ing (physical training) like a mad man. I had only three months before boot camp and I trained hard to improve my PFT score. Eventually I scored 291 out of 300 (80 sit-ups for 100 points; 19 pull-ups for 95 points; 18:40 three-mile run for 96 points) for my officer package to be reviewed by the Board in Quantico, Virginia. Much to my delight, with less than a month before I was due to depart for Parris Island, I was accepted into the Platoon Leaders Class Officer Program, which involved going to Officer Candidate School in Quantico for two, six-week summer sessions during my junior and senior years of college.

In the summer of 1997, the day for Officer Candidate School (OCS) finally arrived, and I boarded a plane in Orlando, Florida, bound for Quantico, Virginia. The first days were nothing like my expectations. Daniel's boot camp stories from Parris Island didn't align at all with my initial exposure to OCS. We were tied up in administrative in-processing tasks like getting another physical, sitting through classes, and taking a urinalysis. Peeing in a cup with someone literally standing right beside you watching was something I never got used to. By the third day, when no one had shaved our heads or screamed at us, I was wondering what was going on. I was getting a little bored.

Then, when five hundred of us were sitting in a large auditorium for yet another class on heat-related injuries and how to avoid them, it happened. In the middle of the lecture, the doors flew open, and a pack of ravenous wild dogs ran inside. These were the legendary men known as drill instructors. They turned off the lights and knocked over canteens and threw tables and chairs around in the darkness. Finally, I got the yelling and screaming and intimidation I had been bracing myself for. We had known the earthquake was coming, and now the shockwaves had arrived.

"Get outside!" they screamed at the top of their voices. "Get outside! Get outside! Grab your trash and get outside!"

Unable to see anything, I grabbed my two sea bags and the rest of my "trash" and assembled outside. Then they marched us to squad bays a half-mile across the parade deck, which was an asphalt surface for formation marching with rifles. The squad bays were multi-story brick dormitories with no privacy, similar to barracks, where we would live during the training. My platoon was on the third deck. Bunk bed "racks" stood against the sides of the long, rectangular squad bay with an open aisle called a runway that split them down the middle.

The drill instructors (DIs) started screaming, "Dump all your trash on the deck. All of it right now! Nope, too slow! Put all your trash back in your sea bags! Ten, nine, eight, five, three, ZEEEROOOO!"

That first day in the squad bay we learned that as soon as we heard a drill instructor count down from ten, usually skipping over half of the numbers to get to "zero," we all had to stop moving and say, "Freeze, candidate! Freeze!"

They kept telling us to "dump all our trash on the deck" and then to put it back in our sea bags. We played this sea bag game for a couple of hours, and I finally figured out they were checking for contraband like cigarettes, food, pornographic magazines, and anything else we weren't allowed to have.

The drill instructors intimidated, insulted, and got in our faces at every opportunity. One in particular, Griffin, I remember very well. He was a gunnery sergeant from Haiti, thin and muscular with not an ounce of fat on him. He was older than we were by at least ten years, but he was fast. He could do 50 pushups in 30 seconds flat. Gunnery Sergeant Griffin, like all the other DIs, would get right in your face and scream. Because they had been DIs so long, their voices were damaged from screaming, so they modified the pitch. It was more like growling and grunting, but still menacing. And regardless of pitch or volume, the screaming and yelling worked: we stood where we were told, looked where we were told, and breathed when we were told.

One of the most difficult adjustments was learning how to speak properly. We had to use the third person, avoiding pronouns like *I, me, my, mine,* and not talk with our hands.

"Where are you from, Candidate Dietrich?"

"I'm from..."

"I...I...which eye? Your left eye or your right eye?"

"This candidate is from Tampa, Florida," I said, responding in the required third person.

In addition to this unfamiliar, third-person way of speaking, we had to stand at attention when we addressed a DI. I often use hand gestures when I'm talking, so it was difficult to speak with my hands and arms at my side. Gunnery Sergeant Griffin, in his Haitian accent, screamed at me on more than one occasion. "Candidate Dietrich, you think I'm stupid or something? You think you have to use your hands to explain it to me? You think you're smarter than me just because you're in college!" It was extremely challenging to talk like that: all in the third person, with no body language whatsoever.

At the beginning of the third week of OCS, we mustered outside early one morning for physical training. I was looking forward to this PT session because I had practiced the obstacle course for months back in Florida, and I was ready for that rope at the end. The second obstacle on the course involved jumping up and grabbing a pull-up type bar and flipping over it. I had practiced this countless times at home and I was very good at it. I confidently ran up to the bar and jumped with my arms extended over my head and proceeded to flip over it by doing what they called a "college boy roll." Just then, with my arms extended and shoulders beside my ears, I felt and heard my right shoulder rip. The pain was instant and severe, and I dropped off the bar. Just then, a DI ran over to me and started screaming, "Get back on that bar, candidate!"

I hesitated, knowing the force of the pain that would hit me if I got back on the bar. Then he shouted, "Oh, are you refusing to train? Are you quitting?"

I shouted back, "No, Sergeant Instructor!"

I jumped up and grabbed the bar again, and my shoulder was on fire, burning with pain. I did the only thing I could do: I dropped off again.

He screamed at me. "Are you hurt, Candidate, or are you in pain? If you're hurt, I'll send you to see the corpsman. If you're just in pain, then good-to-go! Pain is just weakness leaving the body. So which is it?"

I instantly replied, "This candidate is just in pain, Sergeant Instructor!"

Somehow, and I don't really know how, I made it through the obstacle course and even up the rope. That night in my rack, I couldn't raise my right arm over my head. I just lay there and asked God to heal my shoulder. There's no way, I thought to myself, that I'm going to be able to go three more weeks with my shoulder like this. When I woke up the next morning, though, it felt worse.

The prayer I sent up while I was struggling with pain must have been born of instinct, because I was not close to God at all that summer. I wasn't spending time with Him, I wasn't praying to Him, I wasn't reading His Word. For me to lie there in my rack and ask Him to heal my shoulder so I would not be sent home was like a little kid right before Christmas. Once a year, he asks Santa Claus to deliver his favorite toys to his living room; but the rest of the year, he barely thinks of the man in the red suit at all. I was like that little kid: I wanted the gift of a healthy shoulder, and I wanted the Lord to deliver it to me at OCS. But most of the time I was not thinking of the Lord at all. No one could point to me and claim I made it a priority to get to know Him.

My goal was to keep from washing out of OCS, which was very different from enlisted boot camp. In enlisted boot camp, they want you to graduate; in OCS, they are trying to get rid of you. At boot camp, if you're out of shape, they put you in Physical Conditioning Platoon (PCP) until you're ready to try it again in a different platoon. If you're injured, you go to Medical Rehabilitation Platoon (MRP) until you're healed up. At OCS, though, they had a 30% minimum attrition rate: it was a quota. Starting on day one, the DIs began to weed through 30% of us and send us packing. Much of that was for lack of physical ability, but the remainder was for "a lack of leadership potential." If you cracked under the pressure, you were kicked out and sent home. And to meet the quota, they created super-stressful situations to get us to fall apart.

As we did our warm-up stretches the next day, including arm circles, I knew I was in trouble. I could barely raise my right arm to the side more than waist high. Doing a windmill arm circle high enough so that my shoulders touched my ears seemed downright impossible.

One of the DIs picked up on my struggle right away and ran over to me, ready for battle. "Are you sandbaggin', Dietrich? Touch your ears! Touch your ears!"

"Aye, aye, Sergeant Instructor!"

I closed my eyes, gritted my teeth, and grunted as I swung my right arm as high as I could. It hurt like crazy. After a few seconds he turned his attention elsewhere and I quickly lowered my right arm to relieve the searing pain. Going to sick call wasn't an option: I didn't want to get dropped for being injured as many of the candidates had already been. I was determined to make it through.

Over half of my platoon at OCS were already Marines, referred to as "prior-enlisted." They had already been to boot camp and knew all the things I had no clue about, such as how to make a rack, how to shine boots, how to march and perform rifle manual, and how to read a contour map. Even the little things were a mystery to me. For example, who knew that the different colored lenses for the moonbeams (flashlights) were in the bottom "secret compartment" that you had to unscrew to open?

I'll be honest: I struggled through this first, six-week session of OCS in just about every way possible. I hadn't worn deodorant for four weeks because the extreme heat combined with my antiperspirant had clogged my sweat glands. My lymph nodes were swollen to the size of golf balls. I was pathetic: bloody blisters on the heels of both feet, a bad shoulder, and a stench that could raise the dead. I couldn't wait for it to be over.

Finally, graduation day came. The entire battalion of candidates was formed on the grinder as family and friends waited for us to pass and review by them. As we marched at right shoulder arms toward the bleachers where our families were seated, a light breeze blew across my face. Suddenly, the sweet smell of someone's perfume hit my nostrils like the force of a rushing wind. It was intoxicating. I just closed my eyes and marched onward, breathing deeply. After enduring my nasty body odor and the close-quartered, foul reek of fifty other guys for six weeks, I remember thinking, "This is the most pleasant thing I've ever smelled in my life!"

I returned to civilian life in central Florida for my final year of engineering school as a changed young man. I replayed the aspects of OCS that gave me problems and determined that the following summer would not have the same outcome. Now I knew what to expect, and I trained harder than ever before. For example, I would intentionally run in the hottest part of the mid-Florida humid heat. I ran with boots and a loaded pack. I wore my combat boots everywhere, even to work. I did pull-ups and climbed the rope in my back yard so much that I had the calluses of a steel worker. I practiced marching, map reading, and I even memorized the cadences the DIs used.

That year flew by, and I felt well-prepared for the final, six-week session of OCS called "Seniors." This time around, I wanted to excel.

We hit the ground running during Seniors, without the administrative work of the previous summer. The first thing we did, after the resident beautician styled our hair into a fine-looking buzz cut, was to run a PFT. This time, I ended up with the highest score in my squad of 13 candidates, and the second highest in the platoon. Unlike the previous year, everything seemed to come easily this time, and I found myself helping the other candidates through things I had struggled with before.

One of the problems that had demoralized me the previous summer was peer evaluations, known as "spear evals." This involved ranking all of the other candidates in our squad from one to twelve. If you fell in the top three or the bottom three, you had to talk to the platoon sergeant and platoon commander. During Juniors, we did four peer evals, and every time, I was ranked in the bottom three, forced to convince the DI and my captain not to send me home for a lack of "leadership potential." This time, I was ranked number one, so my visit to the DI and to the captain was much more pleasant than it had been the summer before.

My favorite DI, Staff Sergeant Tank, gave me the ultimate compliment when we were out on a formation run one morning. He was calling cadence as we ran. When he reached the end of his ditty, he called me out. "Candidate Dietrich, come on out. We wanna hear your girl-scout shout. Take it on the left foot – mighty, mighty left foot. Take it!"

Then I shouted, "I got it!"

Being called out to lead cadence on a formation run was quite an honor, and to my knowledge, the only time that a DI had done that. I led the platoon in a cadence run for the next few miles – what a thrill! And after my disappointing performance in Juniors, this honor meant even more.

Instead of flying home from OCS this time, I got to drive home with Mary. We spent fourteen hours together traveling through five states, catching up and planning our wedding. Mary and I got married on my dad's birthday, 28 August 1998. We returned from our honeymoon at the beach in New Smyrna Beach, Florida, and began a new chapter of our lives together.

Chapter Seven

Reliving the Terror

God doesn't want our success; He wants us. – Charles Colson

27 SEPTEMBER 2002 CAMP LEJEUNE, NORTH CAROLINA

NCIS had to start the investigation somewhere, and they started with us. Since it appeared that a rigger had tampered with the chutes, we were the logical starting point.

We drove from the paraloft to the NCIS building, another rusty brown brick structure by the 2nd Marine Division Headquarters. When we arrived, I got a headcount and proceeded inside. As we went in, I remember thinking, "Is this a bad dream? I cannot believe this is happening." It was too much to take in: NCIS was conducting an official investigation to determine who in my platoon was the Judas, the one who had decided to betray his fellow Marines.

The first thing we did was to stand in line to get fingerprinted and to have blood drawn for DNA testing. After they corralled us through this process, they directed us to a large conference room just down the hall. We found seats around a large briefing table and an NCIS investigator addressed the group.

"What we're going to do now is to have you all write statements about the day of the parachute incident. Think back to last Saturday and write down every detail from that day that you can remember," he told us. "Start with when you woke up that morning and end with when you hit the rack that evening. Include as much detail as you can remember about that day."

As I looked at the blank sheets of paper waiting on the table in front of me, my first thought was, "Man! This is going to take me forever. I was up for nearly twenty-four hours straight that day, and it was non-stop action."

I began to write my statement, starting with the early morning hours at the paraloft and progressed to the point at which I had jumped out of the C-17. I recorded my experience in the air as I looked up and realized that my parachute canopy was missing, and I saw only the 30 cut suspension lines flapping in the wind. Then, as I wrote out details of the terror of that jump, the room started closing in on me. My face was running with sweat; I couldn't get enough oxygen into my lungs. What was happening? I needed to maintain my bearing and remain calm because every one of my Marines was sitting at the table with me, but writing this statement was hitting me hard. Recounting the events of the parachute incident and getting them down on paper was like reliving the experience. I felt the shock of seeing the olive drab lines beat against the endless blue sky; I felt the panic of trying to pull my reserve. It was eerie and extremely uncomfortable, as though the fall were happening all over again. One thing was certain: I couldn't keep writing. I turned my stack of papers over on the table and stood up. I walked over to the NCIS investigator and said, "I need to hit the head. I'll be right back."

In the bathroom down the hall, I leaned over the sink and splashed cold water on my face. I tried to compose myself, but the events of that day kept flooding back and becoming too real. I stood there, gripping the sides of the sink, and looked at myself in the mirror. "Lord," I prayed intently, "please help me. I feel like I'm about to lose it." I took several deep breaths and shook my head to clear the panic. After a few minutes, I returned to the conference room in a better frame of mind, but certainly not a hundred percent. In hindsight, I realize I might have been experiencing what the military calls Post Traumatic Stress Disorder (PTSD). The Lord definitely answered my prayer, though, because I never had a repeat of that episode, not even after some frantic situations in Kuwait and Iraq.

Back in the conference room, I was able to finish my account of the severed lines. Although we were prepared to be grilled at length on the day the chutes were sabotaged, NCIS took our statements and dismissed us. We went back to the paraloft and continued deployment preparation, and I was relieved to find out that the Marines had started sleeping in the barracks again after a couple of weeks.

My quick prayer in the head in the middle of filling out the questionnaire was answered, and today, I have to say I'm surprised it was. God doesn't owe humans anything, and He certainly didn't owe me an answer that morning. Once, years before, in high school, I had asked Him to come in and take charge of my life, but I'm afraid limited access was all He had received since then. I remember sitting in chapel one day when Pastor Baldwin asked us a pointed question: "If you were to die today, are you absolutely sure, without a shadow of a doubt, that you would go to heaven?" Just when I had reassured myself that he wasn't really speaking to *me*, his words began to strike a nerve. Pastor Baldwin's speaking voice was somewhat scratchy, like the sound of an old drill instructor, and somehow that gravelly tone made his words even more urgent. He leaned over the podium and started talking about sin and about a huge gulf that divided me and God. What separated us, he explained, was my sin.

"Has there ever been a time when you acknowledged the fact that you've sinned against a Holy God?" he said, looking out into the crowd of students. He paused, waiting for us all to think about that question.

I clearly understood what sin meant. Pastor Baldwin gave us some examples of sin: things like cheating on a test and lying. I knew that those things were wrong and that I was guilty of both of them. Then he started talking about something I didn't recall hearing before: a place that the Bible calls Hell. We were all listening very intently by this time. Hell was frightening. Pastor Baldwin told us, "If you say 'no' to Jesus and the free gift of salvation that He offers, if you die without asking His forgiveness, if you die without Jesus as your Savior . . . the Bible says that you will go to a place called Hell. Jesus doesn't want anyone to go there, and that's why God offered His only Son as a sacrifice for you, and for me. He wants to take your sin away from you. Jesus took the punishment on Himself that you and I deserve. Jesus wants to have a personal relationship with you."

Obviously, none of us wanted to go to Hell. We grew very quiet as he went on to explain how the Bible describes Hell: a place where there's weeping and gnashing of teeth . . . a place of fire and brimstone and burning sulfur . . . a place of complete darkness. Pastor Baldwin then closed his sermon and invited anyone who wanted Jesus to be their Savior to walk up to the front of the auditorium.

All these years later, I still remember exactly where I was sitting: on the left side of the auditorium, on the first row of seats in that section. I sat there in my hard theater seat, very ill at ease, and I began to sweat. I knew Pastor Baldwin was speaking directly to me, but I sidestepped the challenge by trying to persuade myself that I must already be a Christian.

Then Pastor Baldwin continued. "Maybe you have some doubts. Maybe you're not 100% sure that you are a Christian. Don't leave here today without knowing for sure. Today is the day you can get it settled once and for all."

I was astonished. How could he know what I was thinking? Was he reading my thoughts? He seemed to be able to detect the argument going on inside my head. Now, years after that high school chapel meeting, I understand what I couldn't figure out then: the Holy Spirit, the real but invisible Presence of God, was guiding Pastor Baldwin's words to show me I needed to get things settled with Jesus. I definitely felt something unusual, some need to do something, but when the service ended I was still in my seat. Even with that extraordinary sense that something important was happening, I couldn't bring myself to accept His offer. All I had to do was stand up and walk to the front. But I didn't do it.

For the remainder of the week, I had a difficult time thinking of anything else. Those words kept coming back: *If you were to die today, are you absolutely sure, without a shadow of a doubt, that you would go to heaven?*

I wrestled with the question over and over, but I found no peace of mind when I would answer "yes," because I wasn't sure. I wasn't sure at all. At last, the school week drew to an end, but I was still thinking hard, rehashing the whole chapel service. The guilt of my sin was very clear, and so heavy that I could barely think straight. I knew I had done the things Pastor Baldwin mentioned, and I knew they were wrong. I knew they were wrong enough to keep me out of heaven.

That Saturday morning, I woke up and began my day, just hanging around the house as usual, trying to avoid doing my homework. But my thoughts kept returning to the same nagging question: *If you were to die today, are you absolutely sure, without a shadow of a doubt, that you would go to heaven?*

Suddenly, the pressure became more than I could take, and I had an overwhelming urge to take a shower. As the steam rose and the water ran over my face, I felt as though Jesus Himself were there, and I started talking to Him like I would talk to a friend.

"Lord," I said, searching for the right words, "I . . . I'm not sure if I'm saved or not, but I want to know. I believe that You sent Your Son to die for me. Right now I ask You to forgive me, and . . . and to save me." The words were simple and plain; nothing elaborate or fancy. But then, something happened; as I got out of the shower, I felt completely different. The weight of worry that I had been carrying for a week suddenly vanished. It reminded me of the main character in John Bunyan's book *Pilgrim's Progress.* Bunyan tells of the big "burden" that Christian had to carry; the load weighed so much that at one point, he almost sank down into a bog. One day, though, it dropped off. Christian explained it this way: "Why, I went but a little farther, and I saw One, as I thought in my mind, hang bleeding upon a tree; and the very sight of him made my burden fall off my back." That's how I felt when I asked Jesus Christ to be my Lord and Savior that day in the shower: the heavy weight I'd been carrying was gone. I couldn't believe what a difference it made. I felt great! I had a smile on my face from ear to ear, and I stood there dripping wet saying over and over again, "Thank You...thank You...thank You." While I was in the shower washing my body physically, the Maker of Heaven and Earth was cleansing me spiritually. I remember that day as if it happened yesterday. It was the best day of my life.

Now, over twenty-five years later, I can answer "yes" with confidence to the question that haunted me back then: *If I were to die today, am I absolutely sure, without a shadow of a doubt, that I would go to heaven?* Yes, I am absolutely sure. Not because of anything that I have done to deserve a place in heaven, but because of God's endless mercy (Titus 3:3-5).

My new life of getting to know Jesus began much like a newborn baby's life begins. At first, the infant is unable to do much of anything without help. Slowly, though, over time, the baby begins to crawl, then walk, and then run. Soon he is eating solid food. And that is what happened to me. Learning more about God and how He wanted me to live was a gradual thing. During the next few years, I began reading the Bible and discovering more about the meaning behind the stories and principles. And I did grow spiritually in some areas; I could see a difference. In many other ways, though, I began heading down a negative path toward overconfidence that was anything but pleasing to the Lord. Instead of building on that new relationship with my Creator, I let it trail off. During the sabotage investigation, I felt an uneasy distance from God rather than the closeness I needed to handle all the questions, the tension, and the unrest in my platoon.

Before long, as the days progressed, the inevitable happened: the news media caught wind of the sabotage. The Jacksonville newspaper contacted the Marine Corps Base's Public Affairs Office and wanted to conduct an interview with me and some of my Marines. To my surprise, our Public Affairs Office agreed.

The Battalion Executive Officer (XO), Lieutenant Colonel Simon, called me and said, "We think it's a good idea to go ahead and give the media information we want them to have instead of having speculation and false reports in the papers. Just be honest with them, Dietrich. If they ask you specific questions about the investigation, tell them that NCIS is handling the investigation and all of the details of the case. Focus on the positive. Emphasize that no one was seriously injured, a result of high-caliber Marine Corps training."

Although we didn't know it at the time, one Marine did sustain serious injuries: Chief Warrant Officer Puller. He had landed on his side because he was badly oscillating as he descended to the ground under his reserve parachute. They would later attempt surgery on his shoulder at the Naval Hospital on Camp Lejeune, but after the surgeons took one look at it, they closed him up. Puller was sent to Bethesda Naval Hospital, where he would eventually have total reconstructive shoulder surgery.

With that okay from the XO, I did the interview. We met the reporter behind the paraloft where we conducted our pre-jump training, which consists of drills such as practicing falling on the ground under the canopy and hooking up our static lines to the overhead anchor line cable inside a mock airplane fuselage.

After the interview and the subsequent article came out in the local newspaper, the news started to spread like wildfire. By the following week, it had gone viral: sabotaged parachutes were on all of the local television new stations, in newspapers across the country, on CNN, and in the *Marine Corps Times*. I even got a call from *Good Morning America* with a request from Diane Sawyer to do an interview with me. The worst-case scenario had happened: the parachute incident had blown sky-high and the media were feeding on it like sharks.

CHAPTER EIGHT

My Familiar Friend

Reputation is what men and women think of us; character is what God and the angels think of us. – Thomas Paine

30 SEPTEMBER 2002 CAMP LEJEUNE, NORTH CAROLINA

Getting a call from a national news program was astonishing, but I didn't take much time to consider the *Good Morning America* interview request. I told them I wasn't interested. In fact, I was directed by my command not to talk to any media without their approval.

Local news, though, was full of details on the event. On 30 September, the *Winston-Salem Journal* reported that three jumpers had to use their reserve chutes "as they fell from the sky." Local news outlet WRAL posted an account on 1 October, quoting the Camp Lejeune Public Affairs Officer as saying that three of us "experienced a total malfunction of their parachute[s]." In a follow-up posting on 4 October, they quoted me saying, "My first thought was 'you have a total malfunction' and from the rest, it was like a blur, almost like muscle memory." I refrained from giving any reporter information on my reserve chute problems; the Marine Corps had directed me to focus on the fact that no one, as we thought at that time, was seriously hurt.

1 OCTOBER 2002 CAMP LEJEUNE, NORTH CAROLINA

Wearing gold wings on my chest, the symbol of a parachute jumper, was a badge of honor. The jumper's emblem was the envy of most other Marines. In our battalion, only experienced jumpers in the elite Air Delivery Platoon wore the coveted gold wings, and we wore them proudly. There were literally thousands of traditional logistics officer billets in the Marine Corps that young officers were assigned to, but only three Air Delivery Platoons in the entire Corps: Camp Lejeune, Camp Pendleton, and Okinawa. We instantly stood out among a crowd of Marines as distinctive and exceptional. The gold wings set me and the Marines in my platoon apart.

After all the training I went through to earn those wings, I would never have believed that one day they would become not a source of pride but a source of embarrassment. By this stage of the investigation, dozens of articles all over the country had been written about the parachute sabotage. And as the investigation progressed, the articles and commentaries got more and more negative about Air Delivery Platoon, my platoon.

One morning in early October, I was on base at the Post Exchange getting a cup of coffee. Standing in the crowded line waiting to check out, I happened to look over at the magazine rack by the register. There I saw the latest edition of the *Marine Corps Times*, a publication distributed to Marines stationed in every corner of the globe. Our parachute incident was the front-page story, with the headline **PARACHUTE SABOTAGE** accompanied by a six-inch-wide picture of silver jump wings. The image caught my eye immediately. For the cover, the editors had modified the emblem so that the suspension lines were partially severed from the canopy to illustrate the criminal act. I stared at the picture; it sickened me. Displaying jump wings in that condition was like a sacrilege. Every jumper who had earned the right to wear them held the insignia sacred, and this image was disturbing, to say the least. And on another level, the illustration was incorrect: unlike the picture, with the lines partially cut away from the canopy, we had jumped with no canopy at all!

Suddenly it dawned on me that nearly every United States Marine in the world knew about the parachute incident and the sabotage investigation. Wherever there were Marines, there was the *Marine Corps Times*. They all would be reading about the severed lines and the suspicion and all the ugly details. For the first time ever, I stood there ashamed to be wearing my jump wings.

The *Times* article dramatically described a "manhunt for the possible saboteur, who allegedly cut suspension lines on more than a dozen pre-packed parachutes stored in II Marine Expeditionary Force warehouses."

The reporter went on to note that the "saboteur was intimately familiar with parachutes."

The word *familiar* triggered a Bible verse. In Psalm 55, the writer laments, "For it is not an enemy who reproaches and taunts me [...] But it was you, a man my equal, my companion and my familiar friend" (*Amplified Bible*). This cut to the heart of the crime, and in just a few words captured the fury we were feeling: it was not a wartime enemy who had done this unspeakable act, but rather a man my equal, my companion, my brother, my fellow rigger. *My familiar friend.* Someone from my platoon had done this, and the treachery haunted me throughout the life of the investigation.

The article went on to say that "Marine Corps officials and agents from the Naval Criminal Investigative Service are investigating. Most details remain under wraps." They quoted the II MEF spokesman, who labeled the incident "a deadly serious issue." The reporter also interviewed a veteran jumper, a former reconnaissance Marine. "You could cut a dozen different things in a dozen different places that wouldn't get spotted on a Jumpmaster Primary Inspection," he said, "But I don't know why anyone would want to." The pre-jump inspection procedure, as explained in the article, noted that each jumper is checked out twice "by two certified jumpmasters to ensure the 'serviceability and proper fit' of the parachute," according to the gunnery sergeant responsible for the paraloft. Chutes were dried in the fifty-foot tall paraloft and then packed and stored in the parachute locker. According to the account, chutes could be packed up to six months before a jump, mentioning that most Marines are not trained in packing parachutes, so they trust the riggers with their lives. The reporter must not have known that in the Air Delivery Platoon we have all been trained to pack the chutes.

But the *Times* journalist got this right: "...riggers and inspectors treat the packing of chutes as an almost surgical process. The riggers themselves are jump qualified and may be asked at any time to use one of their own chutes." The article quoted the gunnery sergeant as saying the Marines could end up with any one of the parachutes for their jumps, so they all "want to make sure they're all packed the same."

I was surprised at the in-depth explanation of the process we went through to pack the chutes; the reporter had certainly done his homework. First, as the article mentioned, we check the chutes for rips or punctures. Next, we have 50-foot tables to lay out the length of the parachute. To start with, the chute is folded vertically and then top to bottom. The suspension lines are added with great care to prevent dangerous tangling, which could be fatal. Experienced inspectors supervise, logging in an evaluation at certain checkpoints. Finally, both rigger and inspector write the date along with their initials in the log record book which goes in a pocket in the parachute.

In terms of security, the reporter confirmed that the paraloft is always locked and "access is tightly controlled." He went on to add that most Marine jumpers never have to pull their reserves. In unusual circumstances, a partial failure will take place, with some portion of the canopy blossoming. Even more rarely, he noted, a "total malfunction results in an uncontrolled fall." The article correctly called it on this one: "The seconds that it takes to determine the type of failure can mean life and death for the jumper." And in my case, the reserve almost failed as well, leaving me with only two seconds before I hit the ground.

The article ended with a statement from Marine Corps leadership, who called Marines and sailors "a very precious national asset" and affirmed the determination to get to the root of the crime. So as shocking as it was to have our platoon on the front page of the *Marine Corps Times*, the article seemed to be accurate and fair, which was all we could ask.

7 OCTOBER 2002 CAMP LEJEUNE, NORTH CAROLINA

The media continued to feed on the events surrounding the parachute incident. Another paper, the *Washington Post*, ran a story on 7 October that began in a dramatic fashion: "Lieutenant Michael Dietrich counts when he jumps out of airplanes. The ground speeds toward him, but this wiry Marine officer doesn't move – he just counts and waits. Waits and counts. He was counting the last time he jumped out of a plane, a training jump from 1,250 feet late last month that has shaken this sprawling base at Camp Lejeune with suspicions and talk of sabotage." The writer described my view when I looked up during the jump: "No canopy. Just blue sky and a tangle of flapping cords, leading absolutely nowhere." Then, he asked the same questions we were asking: "Why, for instance, did the saboteur cut cords only on the main parachutes, but leave the reserve chutes untouched? How could someone cut the lines without being detected?" This account also reported that during the interview, crews were reinforcing the paraloft doors for security reasons.

While the media attention and tensions on base expanded, Mary was my rock. She and I often talked late into the night about what had happened, who might have done it, what the investigation was bringing to light, what might happen next. During those days of waiting and wondering, Mary was in fact my only sounding board, because I was not in close communication with God. Furthermore, I was still supremely confident in my own ability to take care of things and preferred, for the most part, to leave God out of the picture. François Fénelon, writing in the 1700's about people wrapped up in self-importance, said that God "cannot, so to speak, find where to put his foot in souls so full of themselves".[4] At this point in my life, I was full of myself and there simply wasn't much room for God.

I was ranked as the number one lieutenant in a battalion of thirty-five lieutenants, and I knew it. In fact, even though I was a first lieutenant, the colonel ranked me in the top five percent of all company-grade officers in the battalion, including captains. My fitness report, completed by a reviewing officer who evaluates performance, character, leadership, and wisdom, ranked me near the top. On the form, a diagram of Marine Corps emblems resembles the shape of a Christmas tree: one emblem at the top, with six rows of emblems underneath, each wider than the previous one. At the very bottom is a single emblem, much like the trunk of the tree. The second row from the top of the tree represents a Marine who is "One of the few exceptionally qualified Marines," and the colonel placed me in that category, ranking me against all the first lieutenants he has ever reviewed. In addition, I knew that I was the only lieutenant with jump wings, and gold ones at that, and I also realized that most other lieutenants wanted the platoon I had: Air Delivery Platoon. I had a perfect physical fitness test (PFT) score of 300, and I knew that everyone else knew that, too. I could run like the wind and do pull-ups and sit-ups like a champ. My peers and seniors also knew that I had worked as an engineer when I was a civilian, and that I was a fairly sharp guy. Because of these things, I was the envy of many of my cohorts, and to say that it went to my head a little would be an understatement. Despite all my success in these areas, though, I tried hard not to come across as an arrogant jerk. In fact, I would venture to guess that most of my peers thought I was reasonably humble. But, deep down inside, I knew, and God especially knew, that the modesty I was putting on was just a façade.

This pattern of thinking too highly of myself started when my brother and I attended a small Christian school in Birmingham. As a student there, I learned more about what God said in His Word, and I can still quote many of the Bible verses that we memorized. But as a new believer, I began to consider myself a step ahead of most of my friends. Memorizing some verses and learning more about the Bible led me to develop a case of spiritual pride. Some people call this attitude being "holier than thou." In *The Religious Affections,* Jonathan Edwards writes that Satan is especially talented in manufacturing the sin of self-confident pride in humans because "he knows the way of its coming in; he is acquainted with the secret springs of it: it was his own sin."[5] So the Fallen Angel, personally laden with the grimy baggage of his own pride, is a master at cultivating that same festering sin in human beings. A disastrously good fit.

In addition to thinking I was more advanced in the things of God, I also began to look down on people who didn't live by the standards I considered high enough. By focusing on trivial rules instead of on Jesus and His remarkable love, I had turned into a Pharisee, nitpicking and criticizing everyone around me. Rather than spending time with the Lord and finding out how He wanted to change my heart, I enjoyed looking for the weaknesses in other folks. I forgot to concentrate on the greatest commandment: to love God and love other people. I also forgot that I had been saved by depending on Jesus and His sacrifice on the cross, and not by learning the Books in the Bible. His goodness to me came from His loving, fatherly heart, not as a reward for all the verses I had memorized. The expression "Pride comes before destruction and a haughty spirit before a fall" has a special meaning for me, because I would end up personifying this Bible verse in a literal, life-changing way.

CHAPTER NINE

A Hair and a Palm Print

Somehow, what's in our hearts, good or bad, is eventually translated into words and deeds. – Andy Stanley

3 OCTOBER 2002 CAMP LEJEUNE, NORTH CAROLINA

As NCIS moved forward with their investigation, it didn't take long to get results from the DNA and fingerprint samples that they had taken. The forensic evidence made it clear that at least one Marine in my platoon was involved in this heinous crime: Lance Corporal Rayvens. As we had all suspected, one of our own was involved. He was a strong young Marine with red hair, in great physical shape, who mainly kept to himself. Rayvens, called "Red" by the other Marines, was good at performing his duties in general and good at packing chutes in particular; he had a reputation as the fastest parachute packer in the platoon. I later found out that he was chosen Honor Graduate at rigger school, just as I was. Although he was a fairly quiet guy, he frequently mentioned his family, and my perception was that he had a large and close-knit family whom he missed.

The NCIS investigators appeared very professional, in jackets and ties; most were in their 30's and 40's. They asked their questions in a deliberately laid-back manner designed to prompt the Marine being interviewed to drop his guard. Although the way they worked seemed to be somewhat casual, the expression in their eyes revealed that the investigators were deadly serious about getting the job done. They seemed to grasp the situation quickly and have unusually clear insight into the thoughts behind the answers they jotted on their legal pads. And they were good at reading between the lines.

In their search of the paraloft, NCIS found one of Rayvens' hairs inside one of the un-jumped, cut parachutes. This might not have been significant except for one thing: Rayvens had never packed that particular chute. Each parachute has a log record book attached to the parachute harness, and that small tan book, about three inches square, contains the history of each chute. Every time the parachute is packed, the rigger writes his initials, and the inspector adds his initials as well. Rayvens' hair was found inside a parachute whose log record book never listed his initials, because he had neither packed nor inspected that chute. There was absolutely no legitimate reason why one of his hairs could have slipped inside that sabotaged parachute.

In addition to the hair, NCIS had also discovered a yellow sticky note inside the parachute storage locker. The storage locker, about 40 feet by 20 feet, was filled with three aisles of long gray metal shelves for storing all the personnel parachutes and reserves. Down one of the aisles, investigators found the yellow sticky note containing serial numbers of all thirteen sabotaged parachutes, and further examination uncovered a palm print matching Rayvens' hand. Between the hair and the palm print, NCIS had everything they needed to confront Rayvens. It was clear that he was a major player in this crime.

Within a few days, the investigators brought Rayvens in and administered a lie detector test. Of course, he steadfastly denied any involvement and unsurprisingly failed the test. On the basis of the evidence, NCIS challenged him with the lie detector results and questioned him about the forensic data. Faced with these facts, Rayvens didn't take long to admit that he was involved, although he denied that he had cut the suspension lines.

During the next few interview sessions with Rayvens, the investigators drew out more important facts. For one thing, he finally disclosed that he had not worked alone; an accomplice had been recruited to take part in the scheme. Rayvens maintained that he had not cut the lines himself: instead, he claimed, he just "popped them open" and that Lance Corporal Connery was the one who cut the lines.

Connery was several years older than the other lance corporals in the platoon. He was a tall Marine who loved music and played the guitar well, and my initial impression of him was that he was a smooth talker and somewhat arrogant. During formation runs and PT, he had trouble keeping up because he was slightly overweight. Connery was sharp, though, and he quickly learned to use his intellect and experience to compensate for his shortcomings.

Despite his ego, I had a bit of a soft spot for Connery due to a short conversation we had about three months after he joined our platoon. This took place after I learned that his brother had died.

"I'm sorry to hear that, Connery. What happened?" I asked.

"It was very sudden and unexpected, Sir," Connery replied, ill at ease. "I'd rather not talk about it."

I didn't bring up his brother's death again, because Connery clearly was reluctant to discuss it. But after hearing about it, I immediately thought about my own twin brother, Daniel, and couldn't imagine how I would feel if he died. So after that conversation, I did cut him a little slack, but not much.

15 OCTOBER 2001 ADMOC, FORT LEE, VIRGINIA

When I stepped on deck as Air Delivery Platoon Commander in June of 2001, I felt like I had moved from community college to the big university campus. It was exciting, but also a little intimidating at the same time. I had worked hard to get here, with jump school under my belt and five jumps on my jump log, and things were progressing well. I absolutely loved what I was doing. The fact that this was my job and that I was getting paid for it, plus an extra $150 per month for jump pay, was astounding. My next step was attending Aerial Delivery Materiel Officers Course (ADMOC) for five weeks at Fort Lee, Virginia, training that was essentially rigger school for officers.

ADMOC was an Army school on an Army base, just like jump school at Fort Benning, Georgia. Military rivalries aside, the Army instructors do a great job in their courses. At this session I was the only lieutenant in the class of twenty captains, and it was great to have a Marine captain from Camp Pendleton in the course so I was not the only Leatherneck there.

Both Captain Comda and I still had our "lead sleds," our silver wings, and we both needed one more night jump to earn the gold jump insignia. As it turned out, my platoon back on Camp Lejeune in North Carolina was scheduled for a night jump while I was in Virginia at ADMOC. Camp Lejeune was 200 miles away, but Captain Comda and I decided to drive down that afternoon and get the final night jump under our belts so we would qualify for the coveted gold jump wings.

We got to Lejeune as it was getting dark, and I introduced Comda to the Marines in my platoon. After we suited up using the buddy system, Middleton, who was the Primary Jumpmaster for the mission, conducted the parachute inspection on Comda and me.

The training mission was out of a C-130 jumping off the back ramp, which I much preferred over jumping out the side doors. Jumping out of a side door was a much more violent initial jolt to the body because a twisting action was required to straighten out after exiting the side door. Off the back ramp, though, you could look out the aircraft and clearly see the drop zone, whereas the side door jump was more of a leap of faith. That night was extremely dark, with no moon at all. We got suited up, boarded the aircraft, and took off. Inside the C-130, the only light came from the night-vision preserving red lights. Comda and I sat there somewhat giddy in the dim light, knowing that we were about to transition from inexperienced silver wingers to gold wingers in a matter of a few minutes. Finally we reached 1,250 feet altitude, the light turned green, and Middleton directed us out of the plane and toward the black of night. Even though this was not my first night jump, it was highly significant, since it meant I would be qualified for gold wings.

We were jumping into Drop Zone Pheasant, the same DZ where the sabotage incident would take place ten months later. After I exited the C-130 and my parachute deployed, I looked down and realized that the ground beneath me was covered in trees, which was not a good thing. Tree landings have killed many Marines because the jumper could possibly be impaled, so I was aware of the danger as I descended. Thankfully, Captain Comda and I both were able to steer our parachutes through a small clearing, avoiding the trees, and landed on the ground as "Gold Wingers."

Flying high on adrenaline, Comda and I had to rush back to Fort Lee to jump with our class the next morning. This last jump would be our final exam in the personnel parachute packing section of the course: jumping with a parachute we had packed ourselves. You passed the exam if your parachute opened correctly and you didn't "bounce," a jump term that refers to a total malfunction of the parachute and typically results in death. We drove through the night, barely making morning muster at 0500. This turned out to be the only time I jumped in two different states out of two different aircraft in the span of twelve hours.

At the end of every ADMOC course, one student was selected by the instructors as the Distinguished Honor Graduate based on test scores, physical fitness, and leadership skills. During graduation, I was presented with my rigger wings and a certificate with a gold seal indicating I was selected Honor Graduate. For a Marine lieutenant to be selected by Army instructors at an Army school as the best among Army officers, and all captains at that, was quite a distinction.

In mid-December of 2001, I returned home to Camp Lejeune with gold wings on my chest and the title of honor grad from ADMOC. I had been back about a month when I received word from company headquarters that I would be attending SERE (Survival, Evasion, Resistance, Escape) Training in Maine. Members of Air Delivery Platoon were considered "high risk-of-capture personnel," so they sent as many AD Marines through SERE as they could.

I was ecstatic about the prospect of going through this training. From the beginning, the two things I had wanted to experience as a Marine were jump school and SERE Training. Having already been through jump school, I counted this chance for SERE as a dream come true. From the horror stories I'd heard of Marines who had already been through it, I knew that SERE was no joy ride; nevertheless, I still had a strong desire to go through it. I've always been drawn to things that push my body to its limits. It's just the way God wired me.

I departed for the two-week SERE training in early February 2002 and missed the first of what would turn out to be many birthdays. Thomas, our oldest, turned three the day after I left, and I hated to miss his birthday celebration. While Mary was organizing a party for Thomas in North Carolina, I was immersed in situations I had never imagined in Maine. Out in the middle of nowhere, we were facing sub-zero temperatures, up to our eyeballs in snow, and the instructors did an exceptional job simulating the experience of being a prisoner of war (POW). I wouldn't want to go through it again, but I'm certainly glad that the Marine Corps trained me well on what to expect in a POW-type situation. At the time, I didn't realize that this training would give me a quiet confidence when I departed for war and the unknown in Kuwait and Iraq. SERE training is classified, so I'm not permitted to furnish any specific details, but it was, by far, the most intense experience I've ever had.

When the SERE training was over, I came home twelve pounds lighter and a bit rattled. Night after night, in my dreams, the enemy would chase me through the woods, sometimes beating me and interrogating me. The dreams tortured me. For three long weeks I would wake up in the middle of the night, terrified. I apparently woke Mary, too; she sometimes heard me yelling in my sleep. I would be exhausted in the morning, and it was a relief when the dreams finally stopped. Back at Lejeune, Air Delivery Platoon conducted a significantly increased number of training jumps and cargo drops. The buzz on the battalion campus, as the weeks went by, was that the possibility of deployment was great. In early September 2002, though, deployment seemed almost inconsequential after a routine doctor appointment Mary had. She was five months pregnant with our third child when her doctors spotted something abnormal on the ultrasound. Mary grew extremely anxious and nervous. "What is wrong with the baby?" she kept asking me, her face tight with worry. "I know something isn't right with the baby!"

I tried to reassure her, but unfortunately, her worst fears were realized: our precious unborn baby had an arachnoid cyst on her brain, a tumor resembling a spider with legs branching off the central cyst. The doctors were very grave, adding to our anxiety, and referred us to a research hospital in Greenville. We hoped this new facility would find a treatment that would restore the health of the baby, but as we sat in the darkened ultrasound room, the doctor pointed out a second, even larger tumor on the screen. We were in shock.

She turned from the monitor and looked at us with compassion. "I want you to be prepared for the fact that your little girl could be born with severe developmental problems, Mr. and Mrs. Dietrich," she said.

We returned home dazed, not knowing what to expect when the baby arrived. How bad would it be? How would we take care of this baby with serious neurological damage with two other small children to care for as well? Why was God allowing this? Corrie ten Boom once compared anxiety to a hurricane, saying that "worry is a cycle of inefficient thoughts whirling around a center of fear." We lived in Florida and knew about hurricanes, and our fears were great. In the face of our crushing worry over this sweet little baby, we did what any parents would do: we prayed. I petitioned God to heal this little life, and Mary asked friends and family in Florida to pray. Here again, the Lord was campaigning for my attention by allowing this dangerous condition in my baby's brain, but He was finding it a slow go, because I still was not the radical, sold-out believer who would follow his Heavenly Commander to the death.

Our lives were battlegrounds on several fronts. First, the baby's health. Next, the sabotage. And finally, deployment. All these things weighed heavily on Mary as well as on me. Faced with these life-changing events, I started reading the Bible again, talking things over with God on a regular basis, and taking my family to church consistently. We were praying earnestly and repeatedly for Jesus to heal the precious little one growing within Mary. Looking back, I can see that God Himself allowed this difficult health problem to come into our lives for a very good reason. Since He knew we couldn't take care of it, He knew we would be driven to the One Who could. Our panic over our child's brain made us rely on Him, deepening our relationship and our affection for Him. Mary was very, very frightened about the baby's condition, and she worked hard at learning how to lean on Jesus during this time of waiting and wondering.

As we dealt every day with our worry over the baby's development, time went on and work continued at Lejeune. My commanding officers were giving me rave reviews, and my performance evaluations were stellar; my rank continued to be at the top of the Christmas tree diagram on the fitness report. The Lord continued to give me favor in the eyes of senior officers, including the commanding general. In fact, the colonel ranked me as the top lieutenant in the battalion, and even among the top three company-grade officers. The Marine Corps divides officers into three groups: company grade (second lieutenants, first lieutenants, and captains), field grade (majors, lieutenant colonels, and colonels), and general grade (one- to four-star generals). So of the officers in my group, my rank was in the top three. This top rank status was a bonus, and that's typical of our Heavenly Father. He savors blessing us even when we aren't holding up our part of the bargain. He was still patiently waiting for me to follow Him with my whole heart.

The day finally arrived for the delivery of our third child, and Mary and I continued to pray that the Lord would heal the baby, even as the birth took place. The words of the doctor kept crawling through my mind: "Your little girl could be born with severe developmental problems." On 3 January 2003, we stood at the entrance doors to the Pitt Memorial Hospital in Greenville with our heads bowed while I pleaded with the Lord to work a miracle for this precious little life.

As soon as Ciarra came into the world, they whisked her away to perform a brain scan to determine the severity of the tumors. We waited, with the tension growing, wondering how extreme the developmental problems would be and how our lives were going to change. Finally, the doctor came in to give us the results.

"Congratulations," she told us with a smile. "You have a beautiful, healthy little girl. We scanned her brain twice, and the arachnoid cysts have disappeared! We know that the cysts were there two weeks ago, but now they're not."

We were astonished. The tumors do not typically vanish, the doctor explained; she considered it a miracle. Mary and I rejoiced together, thanking God for His magnanimous answer to our desperate prayers. Afterward, I walked down the hall to the NICU nursery window, and saw Ciarra getting her first bath. "Thank You, Lord. Thank You. Thank You for healing her. Oh, thank You." My heart was full.

CHAPTER TEN

An Enemy Within Our Ranks

Everyone would have something, such perhaps as we are ashamed to utter. The proud man would have honor; the covetous man, wealth and abundance; the malicious, revenge on his enemies. – Joseph Hall

7 OCTOBER 2002 CAMP LEJEUNE, NORTH CAROLINA

The Marines in Air Delivery Platoon were like caged lions. They wanted Rayvens in the brig, and it was eating at them. Since I had been instructed by NCIS and the XO to keep investigation details confidential, even my senior enlisted Marines didn't know about Connery's involvement in the investigation, and the lack of information was not helping morale. If I could have given the men some additional facts, the tension might have lessened. I received some support, though; for example, my fellow officers were very concerned and tried to encourage me when we got together. Also, when I called my brother, Daniel, who was serving as a series commander at boot camp in South Carolina, he told me that everyone in Parris Island had seen *The Marine Corps Times* article and was watching to see when arrests would be made. As I had suspected, Marines everywhere had their eyes on the case at Lejeune.

At the beginning of the inquiry, NCIS called me into meetings several times a week, tapering off to once a week as things progressed. During one of those appointments, the investigator informally briefed me about the motive that Rayvens had given. "Rayvens told us, Lieutenant, that you charged him with Unauthorized Absence (UA) and sent him to company level non-judicial punishment. He said that the company commander gave him two weeks restriction as punishment."

To bring him up to date on my reasons for charging Rayvens, I described the UA incident. "Sir, Rayvens has been late coming back from a 96 on numerous occasions." A 96 is a 96-hour time-off period called 'liberty' or 'libo' for short. "Sir, his reasons were car trouble, family problems, and several other things; and I warned him that if it happened again, I would be sending him to see the captain. Sure enough, sir, on Labor Day weekend he was late again, and I followed through."

"Well," the investigator countered, looking over his notes, "Rayvens told us that his girlfriend was going through Marine Corps boot camp at Parris Island, and she was due to graduate during the same time he was on restriction and not allowed to leave the base. He said that he asked you if he could drive down to South Carolina for the graduation, but you didn't let him go."

I explained my rationale for keeping him on restriction. "When I wrote him up and sent him to see the captain, I fully expected the captain to send Rayvens to see the colonel at Battalion Headquarters based on the number of occurrences of Article 86 violations. I recommended it. However, the captain showed Rayvens leniency and gave him the lightest punishment there was to give, which was two weeks' restriction. The following day, he did ask me if he could go see his girlfriend graduate, and I told him that it was out of the question. I explained to him that based on the stipulations of his restriction, he wasn't authorized to even leave the base, much less leave the state."

NCIS then gave me more information from Rayvens' point of view. "Rayvens said, Lieutenant Dietrich, that your decision made him furious that he couldn't go to his girlfriend's graduation. He said that he blamed you for missing the ceremony."

Here was a missing piece of the puzzle, something I had already suspected: Rayvens' motivation for the cut suspension lines was a desire for revenge. But something still didn't fit. As I reminded the investigator, the parachutes were arbitrarily distributed for the jump on 21 September, like they always are. "They know that we randomly issue parachutes," I said, "so if they wanted me to get a cut chute, why only cut thirteen and not all twenty?"

He had wondered about that as well. "We had the same question, Lieutenant, and we're still working on that one. He did tell us, though, that he didn't want to kill anyone, but just wanted to scare you."

Even though I had guessed the reason for Rayvens' involvement, I was still taken aback. For a moment, I remained silent, just processing this information. Here it was, out in the open, straight from the men digging into the crime and pulling out the facts: one of my own Marines, a fellow rigger, had cut the suspension lines, with me as his target. The entire scheme, from start to finish, was something I still couldn't quite take in, even though many months had gone by since that disastrous jump. Rayvens had declared his intentions for revenge, so that much was certain, but Connery was a totally different story. He was denying any involvement at all. Since the stories didn't match, one thing was certain: one of them was lying. And of the two of them, I believed Rayvens was telling the truth.

As the meeting went on, NCIS asked me if I had any idea why Connery would join up with Rayvens in cutting the chutes, and I gave them my best guess. "Connery may have had a similar motive. I put him on the Weight Control Program due to his being out of height/weight standards and for being unable to PT with the platoon during formation runs."

Then I explained what had happened next. "Connery was required to develop an official fitness program, and I made arrangements for him to work with a trainer at the base Fitness Center. Connery thanked me for coordinating this for him, and he said that he needed something like that to help him get back into shape. Every day, Connery would work out with his trainer, and I let him have extra time to do that."

The investigator jotted some notes on a legal pad, listening carefully.

"After about two weeks into it," I told him, "One of the other Marines in the platoon told me he saw Connery in the barracks during the time scheduled for his fitness program. I called the Fitness Center to confirm it, and the manager said that Connery had not been in."

I continued, "Later that day, I called him to the platoon office to confront him about the situation. I asked him about his progress with the trainer, and I quickly realized that he had not been keeping his appointments at the Fitness Center."

I went on to explain to NCIS that I had then sent Connery to the captain for non-judicial punishment for making false official statements. The captain gave Connery restriction as a punishment, as he did with Rayvens.

The specifics of Connery's Fitness Center deception appeared to be of interest to the investigator. As he gathered his notes to leave, I got the impression NCIS was even more certain than I was that Rayvens was telling the truth about Connery's role as his accomplice. He encouraged me to be patient and reassure the Marines in my platoon that the investigation was uncovering some critical information and proceeding at a good pace.

By now, though, the tension in the platoon was reaching a boiling point. The lack of trust was quickly eroding the unity of our platoon. The unknown shadowed us: not knowing the name of the traitor was eating at the men all day, every day. One afternoon, two of my best junior Marines, who were also some of the most mild-mannered Marines in the platoon, got into a fistfight while they were in the head. Unfortunately, the fight was more than just a few punches thrown, and the one who got the worst of it looked like someone had stomped on his face. With all the tension the Marines were working under, a clash like this was bound to happen. Something had to give, one way or another; it was only a matter of time.

The Crisis Management Office on base, along with Public Affairs, decided to send the entire platoon through an Anger Management Course to help everyone deal with the situation. At this point, I wasn't reluctant to accept the help, because I felt that the platoon was about to splinter into a thousand pieces at any moment.

One day after this decision was made, I was eating lunch at the chow hall with another lieutenant when fellow Gold Winger Sergeant Major Laughton walked up and asked me how the platoon was doing. I put down my fork and replied, "We're doing all right, Sergeant Major....just trying to keep the Marines busy packing cargo parachutes and getting everything deployment-ready."

Laughton nodded and asked, "When are you scheduled to jump again, Lieutenant?"

I replied, "We're not ready for that yet, Sergeant Major. NCIS is still conducting the investigation, and they've scheduled the platoon for an anger management class next week."

"WHAT!" Laughton exclaimed in disbelief. "Are they Marines or Girl Scouts?" he asked scornfully. "They just need to suck it up and march on!"

At that remark, I bit my tongue and said nothing. With well over twenty years in, Laughton was a hard-core Marine, a former Special Forces Recon Marine who was, as one of my company first sergeants liked to say, "harder than woodpecker lips." I knew he meant well, but he had no way of knowing what the platoon and I were experiencing. As Marines, we are well prepared to face the enemy, but we receive no training on how to fight an enemy within our own ranks; nor should we.

Chapter Eleven

A Glimpse of Cohesion

We are either in the process of resisting God's truth or in the process of being shaped and molded by his truth. – Charles Stanley

21 OCTOBER 2002   CAMP LEJEUNE, NORTH CAROLINA

As interest in the sabotage grew, the unofficial Marine Corps magazine *Leatherneck* joined other media outlets in writing about the incident. The 21 October headline was "Marines Attribute Training to Saved Lives" and the article quoted Valez, one of the other Marines who had jumped with a damaged chute. "It was a perfect day to jump," he said. "I exited the aircraft and soon realized I had to do what I had to do to save my life." Valez, who said he did not panic, "instantly pulled the T-10 reserve parachute strapped around his waist." Herrera, jumpmaster for the 21 September exercise, added his own perspective: "It was very shocking. They'd basically jumped without a chute." As the article concluded, the reporter mentioned my comment about shaking the platoon up: we were all on edge, not knowing who had done what. I felt my responsibility keenly to build back our critical measure of trust.

NCIS and the battalion XO soon met with me at Headquarters to discuss the next steps for the investigation. At this point, I fully expected NCIS to say they were planning to arrest both Rayvens and Connery and put them in the brig. To my way of thinking, this action would bring a great sense of relief to the platoon. All the Marines wanted to get the investigation over and done with so we could get back to the business of preparing for war. I was informed that some of the men felt that if NCIS didn't make a move to arrest Rayvens, they were going to take care of it themselves. Due to the unrest, we temporarily suspended packing personnel chutes and continued packing cargo chutes, and I was watching for any increase in the tension. These comments from the Marines added to the pressure to resolve the investigation as quickly as possible. We wanted this nightmare behind us.

As we sat down with NCIS at headquarters, the investigator opened the meeting with something new. "Lieutenant Dietrich, we've interviewed Connery several times now, and he's denying any involvement at all. We don't have any physical evidence on him like we do on Rayvens. We simply don't have enough evidence to go forward with him."

He paused, and what he said next was startling. "Rayvens has agreed to work with us, so we're going to try to get some evidence on Connery through Rayvens."

I leaned forward, alarmed by this new direction for the investigation. "What do you mean? You're not going to arrest Rayvens and take him to the brig?"

"We need to get some evidence on Connery first," they told me, "and we just can't do that if Rayvens is in the brig. So we'll be working on both of them over the next few weeks."

The decision to give Rayvens his freedom, even temporarily, was troubling news on several levels. Knowing Rayvens would be working side by side with the men after the incident of the severed suspension lines would be hard on my Marines, on morale, and on me. I felt it critical to try to persuade the NCIS team to take a different course. "Gentlemen," I said slowly, "the Marines in the platoon have been watching what's going on carefully. They see Rayvens disappearing from the paraloft for hours on end for questioning, and they know that he's somehow involved in the case. My platoon sergeant is telling me that the Marines are asking him, 'When is Rayvens getting arrested?' I've had multiple conversations with my Marines about the investigation and have been telling them to let NCIS handle it, but the longer this thing drags out, the more difficult it's going to be to control the situation with Rayvens and the rest of the platoon."

They tried to reassure me. "Hopefully, it won't take long, Lieutenant, and then we can put both of these miscreants where they belong. We feel very optimistic about our chances to get critical information on Connery with Rayvens' help, and then they'll both be in the brig."

Unfortunately, the investigators were not only too optimistic about the outcome of this plan, but they were actually wrong. They believed Rayvens was finally coming clean to them, but they ended up arresting the wrong man.

30 OCTOBER 2002 CAMP LEJEUNE, NORTH CAROLINA

Six weeks had now gone by since the incident, and the battalion commanding officer and the upper echelon decided that it was time the platoon made another parachute jump. They wanted to show the media and everyone else that we were back to "normal operating procedures." In fact, in a very unusual move, the colonel announced that the executive officer and the sergeant major would be jumping with us as a demonstration of trust in the Marines of Air Delivery Platoon. They would put their lives on the line, as we would, and trust that their parachutes were packed correctly and would function correctly.

When the decision was made to jump again so soon after the sabotage incident, before the saboteurs were identified and arrested, I didn't know what to expect from my Marines. Based on statements they had made recently, I was concerned that some would "refuse to train" and force me to take disciplinary action against them. This would complicate things for everyone and compound the strain we were living under.

To my surprise, setting a jump date had the opposite effect. There were only a handful of Marines who didn't want to jump, which worked out well because I needed a drop zone crew, so those men would be on the ground. Initially, the timing didn't seem right for another jump, but I must say that the colonel's decision helped improve our reputation and our morale at the same time.

To maintain the upward momentum, I invited the Marines over to my house that Saturday afternoon for a platoon cookout. By this time, we had a little boy, Thomas, and a little girl, Larissa, and we enjoyed opening our home to the platoon. Mary and I provided the hamburgers for grilling, and very few were left over. About two-thirds of the Marines came and we played tackle football in an open lot on the corner near our house, without any pads, of course. Neither Rayvens nor Connery came. During a particularly aggressive play, I tried to tackle one of the Marines from behind, but my middle finger got wrapped up in his shirt as I tried to bring him down to the ground. When he pulled away, he snapped my finger in the process. Then about five minutes later, during a kickoff return, I had trouble catching the ball with my broken finger, and dropped the football. As I was being tackled, I quickly retrieved the ball from the ground, but jammed my pinky finger into the ground and broke it also. Despite my injuries, though, we had a blast. The men seemed to relax and enjoy being together, and we all sensed a release of the tension that had been building up for weeks.

As we prepared for the training jump, we made sure that everything was done perfectly, right by the book. The parachutes were packed and inspected by my senior Marines and secured in the parachute locker with its newly reinforced and changed locking mechanisms. The security alarm system had been enhanced and all of the exterior doors to the paraloft were reinforced as well. Everyone worked hard, and worked together, toward this common goal, because it was our one shot at redemption, and we all knew what was at stake. This mission had to be executed flawlessly.

On the day of the jump, I was nervous. Sergeant Major Laughton and Lieutenant Colonel Simon (XO) had to first go through refresher training at the paraloft since they had not jumped in over ten years. The rest of us couldn't help but notice a definite shortage of enthusiasm in the two of them; they were clearly not keen about being "volun-told"—our jargon word for being "directed to volunteer." I was glad to see that their anxiety about the jump itself was greater than any worry about jumping with my platoon, though, since the investigation was ongoing.

When we got to the airfield at Cherry Point, the executive officer was more visibly nervous than I have ever seen another human being look. I thought he was going to spontaneously combust right after he finished losing his breakfast. His face glistened with sweat and he couldn't stand still; he kept moving around aimlessly. When I tried to talk to him to take his mind off the jump, the XO had trouble focusing on the conversation. After we got suited up, he kept leaving the hangar every couple of minutes.

"Why does the XO keep going outside, Sergeant Major?" I asked.

"He's going outside to smoke."

"I didn't realize he was a smoker," I told him.

"He's not," Laughton said dryly. "He's just a little nervous about the jump. It's been a while for him."

Watching a tall, tough Marine like the lieutenant colonel experience that level of anxiety was hard to take. But there was no doubt that he was terrified, having a hard time getting himself under control.

Overhead, the sky was extremely overcast, with fog still visible at noon. With our parachutes on our backs and photographers and reporters standing by to capture the action, we waited in the hangar a couple of hours for the weather conditions to clear. Eventually, the news crew left to drive out to the DZ for some shots of our jump. Instead of clearing, though, the conditions got worse, so the decision was made to cancel the jump due to a low ceiling and poor visibility.

The XO cracked a Mona Lisa smile when I told him the jump was cancelled. I'll never forget the look of pure relief on his face. Actually, I was a little relieved myself, because I could barely bend the middle finger on my right hand that I had broken a week before playing football with the Marines. It was still black and blue, and so swollen that it would have been tough pulling my reserve if I had another malfunction.

Even though we didn't jump that day because the mission was cancelled, I considered the event a success. I was proud of the platoon, and they had worked hard and well together. They showed great teamwork, and glimpses of the cohesion we had enjoyed before the incident were starting to show.

Despite the fractured trust resulting from the parachute sabotage, we still regarded the Marine Corps as a career of pride. One man's mistake did not trash the proud history of the finest fighting machine in the world, a strong military presence "where uncommon valor was a common virtue." Every day on the base we drove past the life-sized bronze statue of Lieutenant General John Lejeune, who was the 13th Commandant of the Marine Corps. Our base in North Carolina bears his name. When we passed this statue, we saw the likeness of a man who was honored for his service by France, who led the Army's 2nd Infantry Division in World War I, and who was called "the greatest Leatherneck" for his 40 years of unparalleled service in the Marine Corps. His was a story of tradition, service, and honor, and it never failed to inspire us to give our best as well.

4 SEPTEMBER 1999 FLORIDA

We were all proud to wear the Marine Corps eagle, globe, and anchor, and I remember vividly the day I was commissioned as a second lieutenant in September of 1999. I was in central Florida, standing in the sunshine on the banks of a beautiful lake in my grandfather's back yard. Mary watched, holding our seven-month-old son, as the Orlando OSO captain commissioned me. I recited the Officer's Oath, feeling the weight of the powerful words: *defend* and *allegiance* and *obligation*.

"I, Michael Dietrich, do solemnly swear that I will support and defend the Constitution of the United States against all enemies, foreign and domestic; that I will bear true faith and allegiance to the same; that I take this obligation freely without any mental reservation or purpose of evasion; and that I will well and faithfully discharge the duties of the office on which I am about to enter. So help me God."

Daniel had received his commission one year earlier, so I stood at attention with my head and eyes straight to the front while my twin brother and my grandfather did the honors of pinning the gold bars on my uniform. It was a proud, proud day for my brother, my grandfather, and me.

6 NOVEMBER 2000 CAMP LEJEUNE, NORTH CAROLINA

I quickly immersed myself in landing support operations, my first assignment as a brand new second lieutenant learning how to be a platoon commander in Beach and Terminal Operations Company (BTO). At Logistics Officer training, the primary focus had been motor transportation, with only brief mentions of BTO and landing support operations, since the majority of the class would be assigned to motor-T units (motor transport). So I had a lot to learn; I didn't know the first thing about how to coordinate Helicopter Support Team (HST) missions or anything about port and beach operations. By the time I had been the Landing Support Platoon Commander for six months, things were going well. For one thing, I was glad to see that the Marines were in much better physical shape as a result of our physical fitness sessions. Also, I had gained a lot of experience in conducting missions and even spent five weeks in the Yuma, Arizona, desert conducting HST missions with them. Within the company, I had developed a reputation as an officer who did things by the book with an easy-going, approachable demeanor, and there was a great deal of satisfaction in my work.

Shortly after our little girl Larissa was born in 2001, there was another landmark day in my Marine Corps career. My good friend Lieutenant Dole, commander of Air Delivery Platoon, looked me up when he got orders to go to Hawaii. For some reason, Dole took a lot of devilish pleasure in calling me "Leg."

"Leg," he said, "you know, almost every lieutenant in the battalion has come to lobby me about being the next AD platoon commander. Why haven't you asked me to put in a good word for you?"

I replied, "I figured it would happen if it was supposed to. I didn't want to campaign for it."

"That's one of the reasons I like you, Leg," he grinned. "Just to let you know, I've already recommended to the captain and to the colonel that you be the next AD Platoon Commander. I don't know if they've got someone else in mind, but I wanted you to know that I recommended you."

A week later, I was ordered to report to the Company Commander's Office. I walked in, centered myself in front of his desk, and stood at attention. "Reporting as ordered, sir."

He said, "At ease, Lieutenant Dietrich. Take a seat."

I sat down and saw that the colonel was also there. He looked my way and started discussing a plan to transition from my current platoon. He said, "You're a little older and more mature than most second lieutenants, and I'm going to expect a lot out of you."

I was lost. I mentally sifted through his comments, trying to understand what he meant. Finally I spoke up. "Sir, I'm not exactly sure what we're talking about."

Just then the captain broke in. "Sir, I haven't informed Lieutenant Dietrich that he's going to Air Delivery Platoon yet."

"Oh," the colonel said. "Well, congratulations, then. I thought you already knew."

I managed to give them the appropriate words of appreciation, but what I wanted to do was stand up and do a back flip. Back in Quantico, before I even knew my unit assignment, I had wanted to be in Air Delivery, and this morning it became a reality. While my mind was whirling with this immensely good news, the colonel said he wanted me to go to jump school as soon as possible, so I could step on deck as the Air Delivery Platoon Commander with jump wings. I could hardly wait to get home and tell Mary that my dream had come true: platoon commander of Air Delivery and jump school all at once!

Chapter Twelve

What a Marine Is Made Of

The weaker we feel, the harder we lean. And the harder we lean, the stronger we grow. – J.I. Packer

4 JUNE 2001   FORT BENNING, GEORGIA

W ith my new assignment to AD platoon, I was riding high. In June of 2001, I departed for jump school at Fort Benning, Georgia, filled with varied emotions, because this was something I had wanted to do since I was a little kid jumping out of trees pretending to be Superman. I was extremely eager to get back to Camp Lejeune so I could get snapped into my new role as the Air Delivery Platoon Commander. I was also determined to show these "Army pukes" at Fort Benning what a Marine was made of.

Before jump school, back when I had been the Landing Support Platoon Commander for only six months, I met the current Air Delivery Platoon Commander, First Lieutenant Dole. He got a kick out of calling me "Leg," and I finally figured out why. I was a "Leg" because I was limited to walking where I was going, but Dole could fly, since he had his wings. Earning jump wings was a big deal to Lieutenant Dole and the rest of his platoon. They were the only Marines in the battalion who were jump-qualified, and that skill set them apart. In addition to having their wings, Air Delivery Platoon had the reputation for being the best in the battalion at almost everything: physical fitness, discipline, unit cohesion, you name it. Air Delivery Platoon was number one, and everyone knew it.

Wearing gold wings on your chest meant you were an experienced jumper in the elite Air Delivery Platoon. There were thousands of traditional logistics officer billets in the Marine Corps that young officers were assigned to, but only three Air Delivery Platoons in the entire Corps: Camp Lejeune, Camp Pendleton, and Okinawa. Lieutenant Dole had the billet that just about every other young logistics officer on the East coast wanted, including me. So I was thrilled to be slated for jump school, which was held on an Army base. Marines attend a variety of Army schools such as jump school and rigger school, and bringing these two branches of service together for several weeks intensifies the on-going inter-service rivalry that's existed since my grandfather was in the Army in the 1940's. At the end of the day, we're all on the same team, but it's tradition to dog each other and prove that your branch of service is the best.

Jump school lasted for three weeks, and I was pleasantly surprised at the level of difficulty. Going in, I thought it would be a cakewalk. I figured that when I finished and returned to Lejeune, I would need to spend time getting back into shape after being on easy street at Fort Benning. I mean, come on; it was an Army school, after all. How hard could it be?

I soon found out that jump school was intense and demanding. The airborne instructors broke the process down into a series of objectives. One goal was learning how to fall correctly, and that skill was quite challenging, as was everything else associated with jumping out of a perfectly good airplane. For practice drills, we worked on a zip line rigged up over a large gravel pit. To simulate the jump, we would ride on the zip line and then drop off into the gravel to practice putting the chin to the chest, keeping feet and knees together, putting forearms up and together in front of the face, and keeping eyes on the horizon during landing. The correct form for landing in the gravel was precise: on the side, with upper torso twisted in the opposite direction of travel. Parts of the training were worse than others. For example, we all hated the rock drills. For this, we would lie on our backs on the gravel, helmet on, chin on chest, forearms out in front of the face, for long periods of time. Holding this position for more than two minutes was very difficult because the weight of the helmet naturally pulled your head and neck back down to the gravel. And we did it day after day. The point of the exercise was to gain muscle memory of the feeling of keeping your chin on your chest as you landed. This part of the jump was potentially the most dangerous and where most injuries, such as concussions and broken bones, occurred.

After the first two weeks of training, it was time for my first-ever parachute jump, the first of many from a C-130. The entire battalion of brand new jumpers was packed into a large hangar on the airfield where we suited up.

Before I left for jump school, Lieutenant Dole had given me some tips about donning my parachute. "They'll tell you, 'the tighter the better,' but you want your parachute harness to be just a little loose," he explained. "Trust me: it'll be a lot more comfortable when you're jumping." Based on his advice, I intentionally left my leg straps and chest strap a little loose as I suited up. As soon as we jumped, I discovered just how serious that mistake would be.

When we boarded the airplane, we were packed in like sardines. Was it ever hot in there! When the jumpmasters started handing out barf bags, I thought it was a joke because it was our first jump. But what they told us next surprised me: they said there's always at least one jumper that "loses his cookies" and always one that refuses to jump. Sure enough, not long after we took off, someone started throwing up in his bag. The sound of retching and the sickening smell of vomit mixed with sweaty body odor in 100-degree heat almost made me grab for my bag as well. I closed my eyes, breathed through my mouth to avoid the smell, and tried to ignore the barfing noises of the men around me.

Several sticks of jumpers went ahead of me, and then it was finally my turn. As soon as the jumpmaster gave the command, "Fifth stick, stand up!" my heart started racing. I was toward the rear of the stick of about 20 jumpers, and as soon as I heard the jumpmaster say, "GO!" I followed the jumper in front of me toward the side door of the airplane. I jumped out of the C-130 and instantly realized I had forgotten to keep my feet and knees together.

I remember thinking, "Man, my legs were apart when I jumped out... that's not good...oh, wait, I'm supposed to be counting, 'one thousand, two thousand, three thousand.'"

Just then, my parachute opened and violently jerked up on my harness as the weight of my body pulled in the opposite direction. As I slowly descended to the earth, I realized in a very painful way just how wrong I had been to loosen my straps when I suited up. The pain I experienced in my groin was something unrivaled to that point. I struggled like a worm on a hook trying to re-adjust my leg straps to relieve the pain, but I could not remedy the situation. The earth was coming closer and closer, and I was frantic to reach the ground so I could have some relief.

Watchful instructors stood on the ground with bullhorns, yelling out commands and words of wisdom as we neared the ground. I heard one of them say, "Alpha, you're running with the wind!" He said it three or four times before I finally understood that he was yelling at me. The airborne instructors called officers "Alphas." In class, they had taught us to position our parachutes so that we were "holding with the wind." In other words, we should turn our parachutes so that the wind was in our faces as we were descending. "Running with the wind" meant that the wind was at your back, pushing you to land a lot harder and faster. It was potentially very dangerous.

At the last second, I tried to steer my WWII vintage T-10 parachute so that I was "holding with the wind," but it was too late. With the current of air at my back, I raced with the wind and landed sideways instead of perpendicular to the ground. I also forgot to put my chin on my chest as I landed, so the back of my head bounced off the ground as I eventually came to a stop.

The airborne instructor ran over to me and said, "Are you trying to kill yourself, Alpha? Are you all right?"

I had blacked out for a brief moment from the impact. When my head cleared, I said, "I'm fine, Sergeant Airborne."

My first jump turned out to be a great demonstration of what not to do: don't jump out with your legs apart, don't leave your leg straps too loose (for the sake of future generations), don't run with the wind, and don't forget to put your chin on your chest during the landing. I had a migraine for two days after that debacle as a constant reminder of how badly that first jump went. The good news was that due to the pain from that first jump, I never forgot to do those things again.

The remaining four jumps went smoothly and were quite enjoyable. The drop zone was huge, and a lot of jumpers were exiting the aircraft with every pass over the drop zone. Probably 25 trainees jumped per pass with multiple airplanes, mainly C-130s, all dropping jumpers at the same time. My favorite part of the jump was the sudden quietness that hit me once I was airborne after exiting the loud aircraft, and the peacefulness of the descent. During the jump, I always looked out over the trees and enjoyed the beauty of God's creation. George Washington Carver once called nature God's "unlimited broadcasting station," and that day the signal was coming through loud and clear. The view was beautiful. I steered my parachute to face the wind and enjoyed the unique panoramic view of nature.

Graduation Day came, and an Army colonel pinned on my jump wings. Back home in AD Platoon, the Marines referred to the silver jump wings as "lead sleds" or "the silver shield of shame," because it was like earning a bronze or silver medal at the Olympics: it's a good and notable achievement, but it's not gold. Gold is the best. In my platoon, about half had gold wings and the other half had "lead sleds" like mine, because they had not yet taken part in the variety of jumps required to earn them. Despite all that, I was finally jump qualified and I was ecstatic. I was no longer a "Leg"!

Chapter Thirteen

3, 4, 6, 9: Get in Line

Knowing God without knowing our own wretchedness makes for pride.
Knowing our own wretchedness without knowing God makes for despair —
Blaise Pascal

2 NOVEMBER 2002 CAMP LEJEUNE, NORTH CAROLINA

Even with the teamwork I had seen during the first jump attempt since the parachute sabotage, even with the cohesion the unit had displayed that day, things in our platoon were still light years away from being normal again. For one thing, there were two suspects, one admitting involvement and the other not, still roaming freely around the base. Also, I was the only one in the platoon who knew the details of NCIS' investigation; I imagine the rest of the Marines had a much more difficult time not knowing what was being done to find the culprits. After all, it had been two months and no one had been arrested. And while the investigation was always heavy on our minds, we were also expecting deployment orders to arrive any day.

I was at the paraloft one morning when the phone on my desk rang, and it was the Executive Officer.

"Lieutenant Dietrich, NCIS is asking about an incident that Rayvens has mentioned regarding Staff Sergeant Jude and Lance Corporal Hartman. I need you to ask Jude if he allowed Hartman to go on emergency leave in order to avoid a urinalysis. Do you know anything about that?"

I replied, "No, sir. Hartman isn't even in the platoon any longer. He checked out several months ago."

"Talk to Jude about it," the XO said, "and then call me back."

"Aye, aye, sir," I said and hung up the phone.

On a regular basis, all Marines undergo random urinalysis. We would almost certainly have a urinalysis either before or after returning from a 96, and sometimes both. For example, a Marine from battalion would order, "Every Marine with social security numbers ending in 3, 4, 6, or 9 come stand in this line." Somehow, without fail, my number would end up always getting called. Having a fellow Marine stand directly beside you and watch while you pee in a cup was always a little unnerving.

I decided to talk to Jude and get back to the XO as soon as possible. Jude was a very likable, out-going Marine who enjoyed reading books on a variety of topics. He also was extremely tall: at least six feet six inches. He could slam dunk a basketball standing flat-footed directly under the goal. Sometimes I wondered whether his conduct with the junior Marines was too permissive, but he genuinely cared about his Marines as people with families, not just as military personnel.

I approached Jude and asked him about Hartman. "Staff Sergeant Jude, do you remember ever letting Hartman go on emergency leave?"

"Yes, sir," he replied, "That was a while ago. I remember he came to me and requested emergency leave, so he could go up north to help his family during a crisis situation. Why do you ask, sir?"

I had been specifically directed by the XO not to tell Jude that NCIS was asking about it. Since it was part of the confidential investigation, I simply replied, "I just needed to know. Thanks, Staff Sergeant."

I called the XO back and let him know about my conversation with Jude. As far as I was concerned, that was the end of the matter; there was no way I could have known that it would rear its ugly head again.

With our previous jump cancelled due to bad weather, Battalion Headquarters had scheduled another jump for Air Delivery Platoon. This time, the entire platoon, including me, was excited about this jump because it would be out of a C-5 airplane. The C-5 Galaxy, by far the largest aircraft in the U.S. military's arsenal, was not normally used for personnel parachute operations. This plane operated more as a cargo and equipment hauler than anything else. With an overall length of 247 feet and a wingspan of 233 feet, the C-5 dwarfed the C-130, which had an overall length of 97 feet. Only a few of the senior enlisted Marines in the platoon had ever jumped from a C-5, and that jump had been many years ago. For the rest of us, it would be a totally new experience.

For the jump we would again be joined by the U.S. Air Force, because the Marine Corps does not have any C-5s in their inventory. I was a bit surprised that the Air Force agreed to conduct another training mission with my platoon, since it had been only two and a half months since the incident with the U.S. Air Force C-17 unit on 21 September 2002, a date I will never forget.

This time, both the executive officer and the sergeant major were legitimately pre-disposed with other duties and were unable to participate in the jump. After the XO's extreme attack of nerves during preparation for the first mission, I doubt he was deeply disappointed he couldn't make the second one. It was set for 5 December, and this would be my first jump since the incident. The fingers I had broken playing football were feeling much better at this point, and it was a relief to see that there wasn't nearly as much media fanfare as there was for the first scheduled jump.

25 JUNE 2001 CAMP LEJEUNE, NORTH CAROLINA

Being in command of the air delivery platoon continued to be a source of pride for me. I had the elite platoon and the job of my dreams. I remember the feeling of excitement after completing jump school: with jump wings on my chest, I returned to Camp Lejeune feeling ten feet tall and bullet proof! I reported to Air Delivery Platoon's Headquarters, called the paraloft, a building used for packing and storing our gear, including all cargo and personnel parachutes.

Stepping on deck to take the reigns as platoon commander made me a little nervous on my first day. Staff Sergeant Domino, my platoon sergeant at the time, had the platoon standing at attention in formation out front. As I rounded the corner, Domino faced about and waited for me to approach.

I centered myself in front of him at attention, and he said, "Good morning, sir. The platoon is formed and ready, awaiting your instruction, sir."

I was not at all expecting this type of formal welcome and was not prepared for it.

"Good morning, Staff Sergeant. Take your post at the rear of the formation."

Domino marched to the rear of the platoon and I gave the command, "At ease."

I then told the platoon I was honored to be leading them as their platoon commander, and that I didn't take that responsibility lightly. I also explained that I planned to be their platoon commander for at least a year, hopefully longer. In the past, the Air Delivery Platoon Commander billet was viewed as a reward for top performing lieutenants. They would be in the position only long enough to earn their gold wings and then step aside after a few months, to give another well-deserving lieutenant a turn.

Unfortunately, the Air Delivery Platoon had acquired a reputation of being a "jump club," and other platoons considered them to be focused on jumping from planes but nothing more serious or beneficial than that. They were regarded as having considerable talent and they got appropriate attention from the other platoons. But as Coach John Wooden once observed, "Talent is God given. Be humble. Fame is man-given. Be grateful. Conceit is self-given. Be careful." Too much talent and attention could lead to conceit, a dangerous landing place. It was regrettable that the elite status of Air Delivery had developed into a negative image. Despite the fact that only parachute riggers and top-performing lieutenants were selected for the platoon, the reputation of Air Delivery was focused on fun.

Certainly, jumping was an important part of the platoon's mission, but the cargo air drop is the most important part of air delivery. Marines on the ground needed supplies in places that could not be reached by trucks and other rolling stock, so air delivery was the only option. The battalion realized that the negative view held by other platoons was not in the best interest of the Air Delivery Marines or the Corps, and Lieutenant Dole had started changing that mindset, focusing on the true mission of air delivery. In fact, he had charged me with that mission before he left. To continue in that vein, I informed the platoon that I planned to do a lot more cargo drop training missions and that I viewed personnel jumps as secondary to the primary mission of honing our skills at rigging and air-dropping re-supply items for Marines on the ground.

"I don't care if it takes me a year to get my gold wings. What I do care about is making sure that we're combat ready to perform our mission when the time comes."

As I scanned the canvas of Marines in front of me, I took at their spit-shined boots and crisply pressed uniforms. They looked sharp. I told them that I intended to make certain that we upheld the reputation of being the best in the battalion – at everything.

"You have wings on your chest, and you're parachute riggers. That makes you special and sets you apart from the rest. We will never be satisfied with being average. We'll lead from the front in everything we do."

Taking a more relaxed tone, I mentioned, "I hear you guys can run pretty fast."

They just stared at me without responding, and I continued, "Very well. We'll have platoon PT tomorrow morning and see about that." There are some common traits in almost all Marines, and one is a competitive spirit. I knew that and I was trying to get them motivated to give their all the next morning on our platoon run.

That night when I got home, I was so excited to tell Mary about the platoon and how things went on my first day.

"Well, I'm so glad you're happy, Sweetie," my wife said, trying valiantly to share my enthusiasm, "but you know I still don't really like the idea of you jumping out of airplanes." That made me smile. Mary thought my work involved danger and she didn't want me to get hurt. I liked knowing the woman I loved considered me irreplaceable. I felt like her hero.

That first day set the tone for my tenure as Air Delivery Platoon Commander. I thought Domino was the epitome of what a platoon sergeant should be. Things were definitely getting started on the right foot, which is actually the left foot for Marines, as all devil dogs know.

The following day was to be our platoon run. I had challenged my Marines and I was eager to see how they would stand up to the test. We mustered that morning at 0600, and I decided to take the platoon on a seven-mile course through some woods behind the paraloft that I had run dozens of times. The course started on a wide tank trail, snaked into the woods and became a single-track trail, and then wound its way behind the brig and back where it began. As we started off, I set a slow pace to get everyone warmed up and then gradually picked up speed over the next two miles. I frequently looked behind me, thrilled to see everyone was still together. Not a single Marine lagged behind. As we approached the last mile and a half, I turned and shouted, "Run at your own pace back to the paraloft. I'd better not beat any of you back!"

They took off like bottle rockets. I increased my speed as well, but not like a rabid dog. In about three minutes, every Marine had slowed to a "recon shuffle" and had just about run out of gas. I then went fishing and started reeling them in, one by one. With about a quarter mile to go, I caught and passed the last one. I arrived at the paraloft first and victorious!

Up to that point, I had developed a reputation in the battalion as a fast runner. After this incident, the news traveled like wild fire, and before the end of the week, you would have thought I was on my way to the Olympics. The fact was that I wasn't as fast as everyone thought, but my endurance helped me run for hours, and it was fun listening to people talk like I was some kind of running legend. It fed my growing ego; I relished knowing other Marines considered me a top-notch runner.

I had been in the platoon about four months, and it was the morning of 11 September 2001. I had taken the platoon out for PT that morning and was waiting for them to report back from the barracks to the paraloft after they got cleaned up. I was sitting at my computer in the platoon office listening to the radio and checking emails. The music abruptly stopped, and the DJ made some sort of announcement which I barely heard. Then he said it again with a strain in his voice. "We're getting reports that an airplane has just flown into the World Trade Center in New York City."

I stopped what I was doing and listened intently for more news. A short while later, to my disbelief, the announcer reported that a second airplane had flown into the other tower. Right then, I knew that something was terribly wrong and that this was no accident.

In the days after that national tragedy, I remember that people seemed to come together in unity and brotherhood in a way I hadn't seen before. This change was not limited to being on base with fellow Marines, but even "out in town" with civilians. Everywhere I went – the barbershop, the grocery store, the Chinese restaurant – everyone seemed different. There seemed to be a greater awareness of the value of life and the cherished freedoms of our country. Despite the horror of that Tuesday morning, Americans stood strong against the enemy.

After 9/11, Mary and I started going to church more regularly, as a lot of people did. One day right after the attacks, we were in the van with both kids in the back seat. We had been talking more frequently about the things of the Lord, and I remember explaining to Mary what it means to become a Christian. Even though we had had similar conversations before, this was different. This time, while we were driving down the road, I could sense the presence and power of the Holy Spirit in a way that I had not felt in a long time; years, even.

While Mary and I were talking about Jesus and His death and resurrection, I suddenly had a strong prompting to pull over on the side of the road so I could stop and pray with her. But I had never prayed with my wife before, and the whole idea made me uneasy. So instead of pulling over and following up on that signal from the Holy Spirit, I kept driving, talking myself out of it. As I was struggling internally, the Holy Spirit spoke to me in a real and strong way. The Voice was not audible, but clear and distinctive nonetheless. *Dietrich, I want to give you something as a gift. I'm going to bring Mary into My Kingdom; she's going to put her life in My hands and learn what real happiness is all about. I'm giving you this chance to be the one to introduce her to Me, and neither of you will ever forget this day. Pull over on the side of this road, and pray with your wife.*

I'm weeping as I type this paragraph. I'm ashamed to say that I heard the Holy Spirit so clearly that day, but I ignored His prompting to introduce my wife to the One True God. I kept on driving down the road. I persuaded myself not to stop and pray because I knew Mary understood that I wasn't leading our family like a strong follower of Jesus should lead. Looking back, I deeply regret that; I missed out on being a part of the greatest moment in her life. It took over ten years before I even shared this story with Mary; I was ashamed and embarrassed to tell her that the Lord was leading me to introduce her to Him that day, but I let her down. Finally, I've reached the point in my life that I care more about my wife's good opinion than I care about the opinions of other people.

But God has His own plan, and He was not going to be limited by what I did or didn't do. As Charitie Lees Bancroft wrote in the hymn *Before the Throne of God Above,* "My name is graven on His hands; my name is written on His heart." God wasn't going to let Mary go; He had imprinted her name on His heart. So a few weeks later, Mary was watching the 700 Club on television while I was at work, and the Holy Spirit spoke directly to her. After listening closely to the explanation on the show, Mary decided she was willing to take the risk and take Jesus at His word. He promised her that He would love her steadfastly and never leave. It all rang true inside her heart, and she prayed with Pat Robertson, a total stranger, and asked Jesus Christ to be the Lord of her life.

When I got home and Mary explained what she had done that day, I hugged her tight. Now, we were on the same page. We were headed in the same direction. I loved her so much, and I was overjoyed that she had been brave enough to make the choice to ask Jesus to be her Lord. The changes in Mary were clear to see. She began reading the Bible on her own to find out what Jesus had said and done while He was here on the planet. She wanted to go to church to hear what God wanted her to hear, not just because I had talked her into it. As tremendous as it was, though, I remembered that I had not listened to the Holy Spirit that day, and I felt the sting of regret.

Chapter Fourteen

Where's That Stinkin' Green Light?

It is about the greatness of God, not the significance of man. – John Piper

5 DECEMBER 2002   CAMP LEJEUNE, NORTH CAROLINA

When the first jump scheduled after the sabotage incident was cancelled, we were relieved to finally get a new jump on the calendar. By this time, the morale of the platoon was much improved, and the unit cohesion we had lost was coming back. As always, we met for pre-jump training and did the mandatory drills for landing in trees, deploying reserves, and PLFs (parachute landing falls). Then we were ready for the mission. While we traveled to Cherry Point with all of our gear for the jump, the Drop Zone crew made its way to DZ Bluebird, about five miles away from the paraloft aboard Camp Lejeune. At the airfield, the pilot and aircrew of the C-5 informed me that they would be conducting low-level altitude flight training prior to performing the jump. This wasn't anything new to me or to my platoon, but this low-level training would be quite intense due to the size of the plane. In this training exercise, the plane flies as close to the ground as possible in order to simulate combat. In a wartime situation, the plane would follow the contour of the land to avoid enemy detection. To follow the earth's landscape, the plane would naturally drop and ascend without any warning, and in a plane as large as the C-5, that would be particularly jarring.

Standard operating procedures for personnel parachute jumps involved getting suited up and inspected by a jumpmaster prior to boarding the aircraft. With C-5 jumps, though, the routine was different. For safety reasons, we loaded the parachutes onto the airplane, but didn't get suited up until

77

after the plane took off. During take-off we were required to be on the upper deck of the aircraft and not in the cargo section; and then after take-off, we climbed down a ladder well too narrow for us to fit through with parachutes on our backs.

For the next hour, we bounced around in the cargo section of that C-5 like marbles in a pinball machine. It seemed like fun for the first twenty minutes, much like a roller coaster ride at Disney World; but after the novelty wore off, we were ready for some stability. We struggled to maintain our footing and balance as we got suited up and inspected. Even though it was December in North Carolina, we were getting warm in the belly of that C-5 Galaxy; and for at least fifteen minutes, my only thought was, "Get me off this airplane. Green light, green light, where's that stinkin' green light!" I'm not prone to motion sickness, but with every breath, I was fighting serious nausea from the unrelenting shifting, and we were all in the same boat.

We finally rose in altitude to 1,500 feet as we prepared to exit the aircraft. I was never more thrilled to jump out of a perfectly good airplane than I was at that moment. I finally saw that green light, and the jumpmaster gave the command to "Go!"

I led the procession of jumpers out of the aircraft, and a feeling of relief swept over me as soon as the cold, crisp air hit my lungs. The feeling of nausea I had been fighting quickly dissipated.

Automatically, I put my feet and knees together with my chin on my chest and counted to four thousand. Unlike the last harrowing jump, my parachute opened right on cue. As I slowly descended to the earth and steered my chute toward the rally point, I realized that God had answered my prayers in a most unusual way. I had been asking Him to keep me from being nervous about jumping again and to let me lead my platoon from the front, with no fear. Then I realized that the ordeal of being tossed around in the C-5 and feeling like I was going to "lose my cookies" kept me too preoccupied to be afraid. Certainly, the Lord worked in mysterious ways before that jump; He used a C-5 aircraft and a lot of turbulence to answer my prayer. I was aware, though, that getting an answer at all surprised me to some extent, because my relationship with God was not strong at that time. The request about my nerves during the jump was more like a "flare prayer:" a plea sent up on the spur of the moment instead of a request made on the strength of a daily, close relationship with the One Who made the world. And while there is nothing wrong with flare prayers, there is something wrong when those are the only kind in your inventory. Even though I wasn't running away from the Lord like I had been, I knew without a doubt that I was still very indifferent to Him.

I landed and then stood there watching the sky as everyone else touched down. With all of the jumpers safely on the ground, I breathed a long sigh of satisfaction. "I'm glad I was finally able to experience a C-5 jump, but never again – that was torture!"

To our great relief, the training mission had gone off without a hitch. God had definitely answered my prayer, and as I gathered my nylon chute from the ground of the drop zone, I thanked the Lord for a successful mission. A week and a half later, we jumped one more time from a C-130, and that training jump was a success as well. Although I didn't know it then, the jump from a C-130 into DZ Falcon on 16 December 2002 would be the last jump of my career. I ended up with thirty-one jumps; the last three of them were anything but fun. The joy I once had in jumping with my fellow Marines was gone.

CHAPTER FIFTEEN

The Whole Truth and Nothing But

For my part, whatever anguish of spirit it may cost, I am willing to know the whole truth; to know the worst and provide for it. – Patrick Henry

5 JANUARY 2003 CAMP LEJEUNE, NORTH CAROLINA

I was still receiving positive reviews from my commanding officers, and my performance evaluations were stellar. Senior officers in the battalion, even the commanding general, had a high regard for my record. In fact, I was ranked by the colonel as the top lieutenant in the battalion and was even among the top three company-grade officers. And a month before we deployed, the colonel reviewed my performance evaluation and added a very unusual note to the comments of my company commander: he checked "do not concur." Although the phrase has a slightly negative undertone, "Do not concur" was a highly positive comment, indicating the colonel's opinion that my evaluation was not rated highly enough. From his point of view, my efforts to hold the platoon together during the intensity of the investigation amounted to a superb performance. He recognized my focus on platoon morale. He knew that as part of my campaign to restore some unity to Air Delivery Platoon, I had planned the cookout and a "brick run," which is a team-building strategy requiring the men to take turns running with a five-pound brick through a seven-mile wooded course. The colonel also commended my leadership efforts in enabling NCIS to conduct the investigation without any vigilante justice breaking out. So despite the fact that my time with God was shallow and sporadic, He was continuing to boost my reputation in the Marine Corps. Unfortunately, rather than thanking

Him for the honors that He brought my way, I was shortsighted enough to believe these tributes were all due to my hard work.

With the date of deployment drawing nearer, NCIS amped up their investigation. They knew that their time was limited and that my battalion would soon be deployed, so if any arrests were going to be made, they needed to make them soon. As the sabotage probe intensified, NCIS took a more aggressive approach, and things started happening as though we were in a Dick Tracy movie: people nervously wearing wires and rooms being bugged, investigators setting up stakeouts and listening in to private conversations with high-powered surveillance equipment. All of this intrigue was designed to get additional evidence and confirm earlier perceptions of the two main suspects: Rayvens and Connery.

Two weeks before deploying to Kuwait in early February 2003, the Executive Officer called me on the phone at the paraloft.

"Lieutenant Dietrich, I need you to have the platoon at the Battalion Headquarters classroom tomorrow morning at zero eight hundred in order for NCIS to administer a questionnaire to them. It's important that everyone is there," he said tersely. "Immediately after that, I want to talk to you and Staff Sergeant Jude in my office about Rayvens' claim that Jude put Hartman on emergency leave in order to avoid a urinalysis."

"Roger that, sir," I said, and hung up the phone.

I approached Jude and told him to pass word to the platoon about mustering at the battalion classroom the following morning. Then I repeated what the XO said, puzzled by the urinalysis question. "The XO wants to talk to us about the whole Hartman thing again after the NCIS meeting is finished."

Jude replied, "I wonder why? Like I mentioned before, sir, I put Hartman on emergency leave so he could help his family sort through some difficult things they were going through."

The additional questioning concerned me: with so much else to deal with, why were they digging into that? What difference could it make?

The following morning, the entire platoon was seated and waiting for NCIS except for Jude. At ten minutes till eight, Jude still hadn't arrived. In the Marine Corps, you learn from day one that if you're not fifteen minutes early, you're late. With Jude five minutes "late" already, I was getting nervous. I left the classroom and walked outside. To my surprise, I found Jude

81

standing by his vehicle in the parking lot. I walked up to him. "Come on, Staff Sergeant! We've got to go. You're late!"

His response would start a chain of events that would permanently alter the course of my life. If I could only go back to that day and make a better choice; if only I had made a more far-sighted decision.

Jude seemed extremely uneasy, and I had a feeling it went deeper than being worried about arriving late.

"Sir, I have to come clean and tell you the truth," he said, frowning and biting his lip. "When you asked me about Hartman going on emergency leave, I did tell you the truth. He did need to go and help his family with a crisis; that part was all true. But Hartman also told me that he had been at a party the weekend before and made some bad choices and didn't want to pop positive."

My heart sank. Jude had not told me the whole story, even when I had double-checked it with him. I angrily responded, "Staff Sergeant! Do you realize the position you've put me in here? You lied to me! What do you want me to do?"

Jude felt so miserable about lying to me that tears came to his eyes. "I'm sorry, sir. I've let you down. I've been worried sick about some things going on in my own family, and it's all I can think about. It's been going on for months, and it's eating at me every day, all day long, and I guess I just wasn't thinking clearly when I didn't tell you the whole story. I'm really sorry, Lieutenant Dietrich, and I know saying that doesn't help a lot right now."

He looked down, and then back up at me. "Things with my life are in a mess, sir. I'm really sorry, sir, but I need your help here. Please, sir."

I didn't know what to say, so I postponed things temporarily. "We've got to get inside, Staff Sergeant. We're late. We'll have to deal with this after the meeting," I said.

Back in the classroom, we took our seats in the rear and began reading the NCIS questionnaire. For the next thirty minutes I sat there, trying to complete the twenty questions, but I could not concentrate: I had a moral dilemma on my hands. When Jude told me he had withheld information about the urinalysis, my first reaction was to wish he had kept on lying so I wouldn't be forced to deal with this new twist. I was extremely upset with him. But I was a husband and a father, too, and I couldn't help but feel a sense of compassion for the difficulties he must have been going through at home. And on top of that, I also felt a sense of responsibility to Jude:

Rayvens had tried to make my wife a widow and now he was also trying to ruin Jude. I didn't want Rayvens to get away with ruining one of my Marines by drawing the attention away from himself to Jude. If I reported to the XO what I had just found out in the parking lot, Jude would be in a lot of trouble. His career would be over.

I sat at the table with my questionnaire in my hand, with all kinds of conflicting thoughts stampeding through my head. I knew I should go ahead and tell the XO what Jude told me minutes ago. But Jude isn't the enemy here, I argued with myself. This thing with Hartman and Jude has absolutely nothing to do with Rayvens and the parachute investigation. Besides, it's not like I can go back and give Hartman a urinalysis now. That was months ago, and he's not even in my unit any more. I wrestled with the two options: do I feed Jude to the wolves, or do I step in and protect him from the Marine who conspired against me?

Eventually, we finished our questionnaires and I walked down the long hallway to the XO's office while Jude waited to go in.

I knocked on the XO's hatch, which is Marine jargon for door. The XO said, "Come in, Dietrich. This won't take but a minute."

"Good morning, sir," I said, "Lieutenant Dietrich reporting as ordered."

The XO came from behind his desk and sat informally on the corner of it, gesturing for me to have a seat.

The XO began with the urinalysis incident. "Rayvens just won't let this thing with Jude and Hartman die, Dietrich. He's adamant about Jude letting Hartman go on emergency leave in order to avoid a urinalysis."

"Sir," I replied, "I've talked to Staff Sergeant Jude on three different occasions about this, and he's told me all three times that he authorized Hartman to go on emergency leave in order to deal with a particularly difficult family situation. Sir, Rayvens is trying to do whatever he can in order to shift the focus of the investigation off of himself and onto someone else."

"Very well," he replied, "That's what I figured, but NCIS wanted me to ask you again. Go ahead and send Staff Sergeant Jude in."

I stood to attention and said, "Aye, aye, sir. Good morning, sir." I faced about and walked out of the XO's office. The entire conversation took less than three minutes, but it felt like an eternity. I had not told the XO everything I knew.

As I walked back to Jude, who was waiting down the hallway, I almost stopped and went back into the XO's office to tell him the whole story.

Something strongly prompted me to walk back down that hall and knock on his door. One reason was our friendship. I had spent a lot of time with the XO due to the investigation over the previous several months, and as I had grown to know him better, a special bond of trust had developed between us because of the adversity we were enduring. He was a fellow Gold Winger, and he had made it a point to support me. I hated knowing that I had just lied to him. But despite that prompting, and despite the strong friendship we had, I didn't tell him the whole story. Somehow, I thought that protecting Jude from the guy who had tried to kill me and two other Marines justified my omitting that part of the story, especially given the insignificance of the event: this was the urinalysis of a Marine who hadn't even been in the platoon for months. How could this possibly figure into the parachute sabotage investigation?

When I reached Jude, I told him, "It's your turn, Staff Sergeant."

"How'd it go, sir?" he asked.

"It went fine. You're up," I curtly replied.

As Jude walked away from me and toward the XO's office, I was hoping that he would come clean to the XO and tell him the whole truth on his own. As it would turn out, that did not happen, and the consequences of his omission were severe.

CHAPTER SIXTEEN

Pre-trial Confinement

The Bible tells us to love our neighbors, and also to love our enemies: probably because they are generally the same people. – G.K. Chesterton

27 JANUARY 2003   CAMP LEJEUNE, NORTH CAROLINA

W hen flatbed trailers showed up at the paraloft to embark all of our gear, the reality hit me that my unit was actually going to deploy overseas. My platoon had a massive footprint with fifty tractor-trailer loads of air delivery equipment: over a thousand cargo parachutes, personnel chutes, scads of metal skids for rigging airdrop loads, and sundry various types of chains, ropes, slings, and plywood. Of the cargo chutes, the smallest ones weighed 100 pounds and were used for small cargo; the largest was the 100-foot-diameter G-11, and it took three of them to airdrop a HMMWV. The Type V aluminum skids we packed functioned as pallets for securing the cargo for the drop, and were designed to slide out on rails in the belly of the aircraft. These Type V cargo drops were for loads weighing from 2,500 to 42,000 pounds. Most of our air delivery gear boarded a ship on the eastern seaboard bound for the Middle East, but of course, the twenty parachutes associated with the investigation stayed behind in the custody of NCIS.

Everyone, including my platoon and my wife, was on pins and needles waiting for the announcement of our deployment date. Mary had three good reasons for wanting me to stay in Lejeune: Thomas, Larissa, and a newborn only a few weeks old. We were both so thankful that I had still been in the States for Ciarra's healthy birth on 3 January.

The Marines in the platoon were a different sort of nervous. A few weeks before we deployed, I remember one of the junior Marines telling me with relish, "I hope I get to kill somebody when we go over there."

"Marine, you have no idea what you're talking about," I said, voicing my disapproval. "The people who hate war the most are the seasoned warriors, because they know there's nothing glamorous at all about having to kill someone."

Although his comment was rather macabre, I thought I understood what he meant. If a prize fighter always trained hard for the big boxing match but never got to fight, his work would have no meaning. If a world class runner trained with determination day in and day out but never got to run the big race, he would lose his desire to keep running. In the same way, Marines are trained to fight and long for the opportunity to practice what they have worked so hard to master. So even though I straightened the junior Marine out, I understood his sentiment. Our approaching deployment was finally our chance to "run the race." Even though I didn't have a desire to kill anyone, I was definitely eager to put all of my training into action and to do what Marines do best: fight hard and win wars.

With our deployment imminent, NCIS couldn't wait any longer to act, and the day finally came when Connery and Rayvens were arrested and taken into custody. It was late January 2003, two weeks before we deployed. For the first time in months, I could sense that the tension and uneasiness in the air were starting to let up because the Marines of Air Delivery Platoon finally had someone to blame, someone to channel all of their anger toward. There was an array of emotions about the arrests. Finally they knew who the culprits were, the paranoia was finally gone, and now they wanted vengeance.

In an *LA Times* article dated 31 January, the two arrests were made public. "Because the cords had been cut so deftly that a routine inspection wouldn't have caught the problem," the report said, "the matter from the beginning was seen as an inside job." According to the account, Rayvens had implicated Connery as the "primary perpetrator." The facts were accurate as far as they went, and seeing it in black and white was unsettling for the whole platoon.

Even though Rayvens and Connery were only suspects and technically they were innocent until proven guilty, all of us in the platoon had already pronounced them guilty in our minds. I was intimately involved with the investigation, working with NCIS every step of the way, so to my way of thinking, there was no doubt that these two guys were guilty. For one thing, they both resented the discipline they had faced, and Rayvens had already admitted his guilt. Also, he had named Connery as his partner in crime. Connery continually denied it, but this was the same guy who lied to me for two weeks straight about where he was going during chow time. I logically assumed that he was lying about the sabotage, too.

The stakes were pretty high in this case. Initially, there were reports that the government would seek a potential death penalty, but I think that was just newspaper sensationalism and not a legitimate possibility. As the lawyers went back and forth during the Article 32 hearing, the charges against both men changed from thirteen counts of pre-meditated attempted first-degree murder to four counts of aggravated assault and nine counts of reckless endangerment. If convicted, Rayvens and Connery would have been sentenced to life in prison without the possibility of parole. Revenge may have been appealing to them in the beginning, but as Aesop once said, "He who plots to hurt others often hurts himself." I had a feeling that things would not turn out well for these two.

There was never a question that Rayvens would remain in the brig for pre-trial confinement based on his own admission of guilt, and for his own protection. There was, however, a question about Connery, so I was called to the brig to testify in his pre-trial confinement hearing. I went through security at the brig and sat on a pew in a small, makeshift courtroom. Based on the severity of the charges, both Rayvens and Connery were being held in maximum security, solitary confinement. Behind me came the sound of chains dragging across the floor, and Connery approached, taking short, choppy steps with his hands bound together in front of him. He was wearing an orange jumpsuit and was held by stainless steel chains running around his waist, wrists, and feet.

Connery sat down at the front of the courtroom, and I looked at him intently, studying his expression. He stared at the floor, with his head tilted slightly forward. The furious, explosive look on his face surprised me; I was expecting to see someone in the pit of despair, looking downtrodden, pitiful, and maybe even remorseful. That wasn't the case at all. He looked like someone who wanted to pick a fight.

The military judge then reminded everyone in the courtroom of the purpose for the hearing. "This proceeding is not a trial to determine guilt or innocence but only to make a determination about whether or not to keep Prisoner Connery in custody until the trial."

As soon as the judge said "Prisoner Connery," Connery gritted his teeth and flared his nostrils in disgust.

After some additional comments, the judge asked me about the details of Connery's previous non-judicial punishment (NJP). By now, I was rather angry with Connery's unrepentant countenance and I described the incident with sarcasm. My arrogance in explaining the NJP and my take on his motive was regrettable; I even referred to Connery several times as "prisoner" during my testimony, having noticed that he disliked the designation. Looking back, I'm ashamed to admit that rubbing his nose in it gave me a great deal of satisfaction. And even more than that, Connery turned out to be completely innocent of the charges, but my sarcasm had very likely contributed to his restriction to solitary confinement.

The afternoon wore on and the hearing ended. Afterward the judge ruled that Connery would remain in pre-trial confinement. So now, both Rayvens and Connery were right where I thought both of them belonged: locked up!

Arrogance has a nasty habit of distorting your vision: it becomes impossible to see yourself as you really are. When I was in college, I had developed a pattern of thinking I was the next Albert Einstein, and I didn't see myself clearly. The Bible tells us that "knowledge puffs up," or as we would say today, "knowledge makes us arrogant." That couldn't have been more true for me. I was taking a lot of math classes and technical courses such as chemistry, calculus, and physics. I was learning about topics that most people didn't know anything about, and because of my big mouth, I took every opportunity to let people know how intelligent I was. Looking back, I imagine that people remembered me more for my superior attitude than for the knowledge I was so proud to have.

During this time, God had tried, on more than one occasion, to take care of this failing of mine, but I would only acknowledge the information and move on without making the change He intended me to make. I remember one situation like that when I was working at the same big box store where Daniel worked when he was recruited. By the time two semesters had gone by, I had wandered a long way from earlier goals of knowing God more personally, and my heart was far from being interested in spending time with Him. An idea I'd had to become a missionary had long since vanished, and my new goal was making a lot of money. I had considered being a math teacher, but since math teachers weren't paid very well, I changed my mind and majored in engineering. Engineers made much more money. God, in His patient way, taught me a life lesson in this area of intellectual pride using a man named Henry.

Henry was a co-worker. He was an older man, possibly in his upper sixties, who worked in the garden center. We had gotten to know each other during our quick meals in the break room; he was a friendly guy. Since I was working full-time and going to school full-time, I would often take my college books to work and do some homework during my lunch period in the break room. On my break one day, I was doing some engineering graphics and design homework. I was struggling with a particular drawing that involved taking a three-dimensional object and drawing it in three views with all of the appropriate dimensions and engineering symbols: top, front, and profile views.

Just then, Henry from the garden center walked in and sat beside me at the table. "Hi, Dietrich," he said. "What are you working on?"

I was agitated by this interruption, because I had been working on this problem for thirty frustrating minutes and couldn't figure it out.

I said brusquely, "Just doing some homework," hoping he would take the hint and go away.

A few seconds passed, and he said, "What is the assignment?"

"Some drawings for an engineering graphics class that I'm taking," I said, deliberately keeping my eyes on the book.

As Henry looked down at my open textbook, he said, "Which one are you working on?"

Now I was getting annoyed. My lunch break was almost over, and the garden center guy was wasting the last few minutes I had. Exasperated, I sighed and pointed to the problem that I was struggling with. What happened next was something I could hardly believe.

Henry gave the problem a quick glance and took the mechanical pencil out of my hand. He flipped my paper over and drew out the solution to the problem. He was able to accomplish in thirty seconds what I was unable to do in thirty minutes.

I looked at the drawing and then up at Henry in amazement. "How in the world did you know how to do that?"

He said, "I retired as a mechanical engineer with Ford and Chrysler. I've done this kind of stuff for over thirty years."

Who would have thought that Henry, the aging garden center guy, had forgotten more about engineering than what I thought I knew? I suddenly had a new found respect for Henry: I realized that he was smarter than I was. François Fénelon, a writer from the 1700's, referred to my reaction this way: "In esteeming itself, it [pride] despises others."[6] And that was my problem: I had dismissed Henry before I even knew how intelligent he was because I esteemed myself too highly.

As I went over the engineering lesson Henry had given me in the break room, I realized that the Lord was trying to give me a lesson, too. Unfortunately, even though I listened to Him when He showed me Henry's superior understanding of those drawings, I was too self-absorbed to permanently change my thinking and my behavior. I was developing a terminal case of pride and arrogance that would take a lot more than one lesson with Henry to cure. And all those years later with Connery, I took it upon myself to teach him a lesson by repeatedly referring to him as "Prisoner Connery" and describing details of my testimony sarcastically. Worse still, I enjoyed doing it. God had begun to show me the extent of my exalted opinion of myself in the break room that day with Henry, but He did not yet have my permission to radically change my heart.

CHAPTER SEVENTEEN

Seven Thousand Miles

Five enemies of peace inhabit with us – avarice, ambition, envy, anger, and pride. – Petrarch

27 JANUARY 2003   CAMP LEJEUNE, NORTH CAROLINA

We had only two weeks left before our deployment, and we were finishing the administrative tasks on the pre-deployment checklist. In the midst of all this preparation, I was notified to report immediately to the on-base dentist, where I had to have my wisdom teeth removed or be considered non-deployable. I tried to reason with them, explaining that I've never had any trouble with my wisdom teeth, but my attempt was futile. Two hours later, I left the dental office with two holes in my mouth where my teeth had been (my twin brother and I were born with only two wisdom teeth). I couldn't believe that with all the work left to do before deployment, I was spitting up blood and unable to eat solid food.

At this point, headquarters had told me that we were waiting our turn for a flight: it could be any day. Suddenly, the message changed. On 8 February 2003, I was informed we would not depart for at least another three weeks due to the backlog of flights and the number of other units scheduled to get deployed ahead of us. One thing you learn up front, regardless of the branch of military you're in, is the "hurry up and wait" game. My grandfather used to tell me similar stories when he was in the army during World War II. Some things never change.

Later that same night, the phone rang at home, and company headquarters gave me a message. "Lieutenant Dietrich, the battalion is scheduled to leave from Cherry Point tomorrow afternoon. Have your platoon mustered at company headquarters in the morning at zero eight hundred."

"Wow!" I replied, surprised. "I thought we weren't going to be leaving for at least another three weeks."

"You know how things go around here, Lieutenant Dietrich. Semper Gumby! I'll see you in the morning."

I grinned at that and hung up the phone. The Marine Corps motto is *Semper Fidelis*, which is Latin for "Always Faithful." In the 1950's, Gumby was a popular clay cartoon character whose green body could stretch high or be pulled a long distance. Kids loved Gumby; his flexibility was his trademark. So when headquarters said "Semper Gumby," I knew exactly what they meant: "Always Flexible." We had to be ready to change our plans at any moment.

The following morning I woke up with a mix of emotions. I was excited that the waiting was over and that it was finally time to deploy. Like the coach who trains his team for the big game, I eagerly awaited what lay before me and my platoon at our destination seven thousand miles away. On the other end of the spectrum, I knew that I was going to miss my wife and kids desperately. Thomas, our oldest, had just turned four years old six days earlier, our daughter Larissa would be two years old in a month, and our little miracle baby, Ciarra, was only a month old. My dear wife Mary knew that for the next several months, and possibly as long as a year, she would be handling everything at home by herself. Although this scared her to death, she was trying hard to be strong for me and for the kids. She wanted me to deploy and do my best without being filled with worry over her and our kids back in the States. She was a very good Marine wife, and I loved her for it.

Early that morning Mary and I stood in the center of our living room hugging one another. I'm not normally big on hugging, not that there's anything wrong with it; I'm just not a hugger. But we stood there embracing on the cold hardwood floors of our house on the base for quite a while.

I drew away from Mary just a little and said, "Here you go, Honey. I need for you to hold this for me while I'm gone."

She looked down to see what was in my hand. Her determination to hold it all together was unbending until I handed her my wedding band.

Seeing my ring was too much. Mary started to cry and couldn't stop. "I don't know if I could handle it if anything happened to you, Dietrich," she said, tears streaming down her cheeks. "I love you so much. I need you to come back to me. *I need you.*"

"God's not going to let anything happen to me, Mary. I'll be fine," I said, pulling her in close for another hug.

"But how do you know that for sure?"

"I can't explain it, but I know beyond a shadow of a doubt that I'll be fine and that I'm coming back." I looked into her eyes, still glistening with unshed tears. "You'll see, Honey. Everything will be okay. I'm looking forward to the day I come home, so you can put that ring back on my finger."

One of the most unsettling things about this deployment for Mary and the other family members in our unit was the lack of a timeline. Battalion HQ didn't know how long we would be gone, and we certainly didn't know either. None of us did. So our wives and families prepared as best they could to be without us for the duration.

My four-year contract was scheduled to end in November of 2003. Mary and I had discussed it, and we both agreed that I would get out of the Marine Corps when I returned from my deployment. She had been a trooper, to say the least, over the last several years, and I thought that it was more than fair. Besides, I knew that if I stayed in, I would have to skip many more birthdays in addition to the ones I had already missed. I really liked hanging out with my bride, too.

Mary woke up Thomas and Larissa, and I hugged my drowsy little kids and kissed them good-bye. I gave Mary one last hug and a passionate kiss. "Don't worry," I told her. "I'll be fine. I love you."

With that last embrace, I walked out the door, not knowing when I would see her and our kids again.

When we arrived at company headquarters, we proceeded to the armory, where they issued our weapons. Officers and staff non-commissioned officers (staff sergeants and above) were issued 9mm Beretta pistols while the junior Marines were issued M16A2 service rifles. The entire battalion departed Camp Lejeune and caravanned over to Cherry Point Air Station, about an hour away.

For several days before deployment, I had not felt well. Over the previous few weeks, we had received a series of anthrax shots in addition to a host of other injections. Also, I still had two large holes in my mouth from my oral surgery. And now, we had yet another shot awaiting us when we arrived at the air station. My symptoms resembled a bad flu, and I wasn't the only one.

In one of our earlier pre-deployment briefs, we were given information about the small pox vaccination given prior to departing for Kuwait. This training brief was specific and contained a lot of graphics to reinforce one of the main objectives. "Marines," he told us, "since you were little kids, your mamma told you to wash your hands after you go to the bathroom. Well, I'm going to now go one step further: after you get your small pox shot, you need to wash your hands before you go to the head as well as after. And here are some pictures to help you remember what I'm telling you."

The instructor then proceeded to explain that the shot we were getting was a live virus on the surface of our skin and that it needed to remain covered. He showed us twenty-five pictures of Marines who had failed to wash their hands and as a result had infected other parts of their bodies with the small pox virus. Over ten years later, I still remember those photographs with vivid clarity.

Dusk was falling at Cherry Point as we made our way, with our two sea bags in tow, to the huge hangar. Almost a thousand of us were crammed into this shelter, and my platoon was toward the rear. We all stood in extremely long lines waiting to receive our small pox shots, so we could board the plane bound for Kuwait City, Kuwait. As we waited, one of the senior corporals in my platoon was hassling one of the junior lance corporals. Corporal Middleton was giving Lance Corporal Dickens a hard time; Dickens was clearly extremely embarrassed. I watched this performance for several minutes and then decided to step in and teach Middleton a lesson.

I walked over to Middleton and said, "That's enough, Corporal Middleton. You just earned yourself twenty monkey-jumpers, right here in front of everybody."

A monkey-jumper is an exercise that begins with the feet shoulder-width apart. Then, bending at the knees, you squat down and grab your ankles. With your hands firmly grasping your ankles, you then would raise your butt up and down, straightening your legs as you went along, and as you counted out the exercise. It was anything but dignified, and my intent was to embarrass Middleton in the same way he was trying to embarrass the timid Lance Corporal Dickens. Aware of the public nature of the order, Middleton walked over to me and quietly requested, "Sir, can I please go outside and do those? That's embarrassing."

94

"No kidding, it's embarrassing, Middleton. That's the whole point," I said gruffly. "These junior Marines look up to you, Corporal, and you're constantly tearing them down, especially Dickens. What's wrong with you! He's an Air Delivery Marine, just like you. You're going to do them right here in front of everyone, just like I said."

Middleton was quite a bit older than the other corporals in the platoon, much like Connery was. As an older Marine, he resented doing the monkey-jumpers publicly even more than the younger men would have. I felt justified, though, because I wanted him to see that we do not tolerate harassment in our platoon. I wanted him to understand that that we needed to stick together and look out for each other, to protect each other; intimidating a fellow rigger and Marine was not to be tolerated. As he complied, few people paid much attention to Middleton due to the level of noise and activity in the hangar. If I had it to do over again, I would have handled the situation differently: I would have taken him aside, talked to him one-on-one, and made it clear that I expected more from him as a natural leader, NCO, and jumpmaster in the platoon.

I didn't know it at the time, but Middleton would wind up at the heart of the parachute investigation.

CHAPTER EIGHTEEN

Nose to Nose

It's easy: You simply follow the trail of your time, your affection, your energy, your money, and your allegiance. At the end of that trail you'll find a throne; and whatever, or whoever is on that throne is what's of highest value to you. – Louie Giglio

9 FEBRUARY 2003 CAMP LEJEUNE, NORTH CAROLINA

I remember the first time I met Middleton. I was in the platoon office at the paraloft. Corporal Middleton sauntered into my office, dropped into the chair opposite my desk and brazenly asked, "How's it going, Dietrich?"

I could not believe my ears.

I instantly snapped back, "Get your butt out of my chair and stand up, Corporal. Are you out of your mind, Marine? You'll address me as 'sir' or 'Lieutenant Dietrich.' Do you understand?"

He back-pedaled and stood up straight. His face was pale. "I'm sorry, sir. I was only kidding. I heard you were easy-going and a cool platoon commander. It won't happen again."

That first encounter with Middleton would unfortunately characterize my assessment of him. He was from a wealthy family, and he liked to push things right to the edge, just to see what he could get away with, possibly due to his privileged upbringing. His parents adopted him from China when he was only three months old, and he grew up in southern California. Even so, he was a natural leader and he was certified as a jumpmaster, one of the most difficult credentials to obtain.

Several months before the parachute sabotage, Middleton had displayed seriously bad judgment before a training mission. I remember that our company commander, Captain Sparty, had just gotten back from jump school with only five jumps under his belt. He was a brand new, inexperienced jumper, and he was scheduled to jump with my platoon. It would be his first jump since graduating from jump school. Naturally, I wanted everything to be executed flawlessly and by the numbers with absolutely no mistakes.

Early Monday morning before dawn, I arrived at the paraloft ahead of anyone else. Middleton was scheduled to be the primary jumpmaster for this important parachute operation with my boss, the company commander. For each parachute operation, three or four jumpmasters usually supervised things, with the primary jumpmaster (PJ) ultimately the one in charge. He ran the show.

After a few other Marines started arriving at the paraloft, Middleton finally showed up. He was late, and this was inexcusable for the primary jumpmaster.

I turned toward him. "Corporal Middleton. Come back here for a second."

He walked back over to me.

"Do you know what time it is, Corporal Middleton?" I said.

"I'm sorry I'm a little late, sir," he said gravely.

"Corporal Middleton, you are the primary jumpmaster for this mission. You are supposed to be here first, making preparations for the jump. What's going on?"

He was clearly uncomfortable. "I. . . I was out late at a party last night, but I'm completely ready for my responsibilities today, sir."

I was furious with this lack of reliability. He should have arrived before any of the other Marines to prepare, and he should not have been out partying the night before, especially since he was scheduled to run the operation from the plane. On top of everything else, Captain Sparty was due to arrive at the paraloft at any moment for his first jump since jump school. I was angered by Middleton's disregard for the safety of the mission and for the need for our unit to be at our very best. Trying to control my temper, I ordered Middleton to follow me through some double doors to an isolated back portion of the paraloft, away from the front of the building. I closed the doors behind us, and I did something that I had never done before and never did again.

Middleton was still trying to convince me that he was 100% capable of handling the operation when I got right in his face and said, "Close your hole, Marine, and stand at attention!" For the next three or four minutes, I literally stood nose-to-nose with Middleton and tore him apart. I was incensed that this Marine would show up late and hung-over and put other Marines' lives at risk. He was not just a participant in this parachute operation: he was slated to be the primary jumpmaster. It was unconscionable to risk the lives of his fellow Marines.

After assigning a Marine to drive Middleton back to the barracks, I appointed someone else to be the PJ. The remainder of the parachute operation went without incident. Later that week, Middleton profusely apologized to me, but he unfortunately took the tongue-lashing I gave him as a badge of honor. I had the reputation among the Marines in the platoon as the kind of platoon commander who was easy-going, but by-the-book as well. I never raised my voice, like many officers and platoon commanders, merely to flex their authoritative muscles. It simply wasn't my style. I hated yelling. So when word got out that I had laid into Middleton, it caused quite the stir among the Marines in the platoon. Later, I heard Middleton joking with some of the Marines about it, saying, "Y'all ain't never seen Lieutenant Dietrich the way I saw him. I'm telling you, don't ever mess with him. You just think he's a mild-mannered Clark Kent. I'm telling you, don't ever push him over the line like I did." He seemed to enjoy bragging about my reading him the riot act, as though it made him tougher than the other Marines to deserve such a tongue-lashing.

Over the next few days, Middleton kept asking what his punishment would be, and after a discussion with my platoon sergeant, I agreed that he shouldn't be promoted to sergeant when the next promotion list came out. When I told Middleton, he had the same look on his face that Connery had back in the brig: not a sense of the seriousness of his bad judgment. Not humble or remorseful by any means. Instead, he seemed angry, furious, and resentful.

Attitudes have a habit of running away from us. We sometimes go too far and don't know how to come back, and that seems to happen to all human beings, not just out-of-control Marines. Back in college, I faced some attitude changes of my own. I was hearing all sorts of things that flew in the face of what I had been taught in high school and what the Bible says is true. For example, the textbook advanced the idea that humans resulted from the

Big Bang fourteen billion years ago and we had all evolved from the primordial soup. But instead of rejecting these contradictions to the Bible's truths, I let it feed my growing ego. My professors were teaching that humans are constantly getting more intelligent. We used to be hunched over; we finally stood upright. We used to be small; we're now getting bigger. We used to be stupid; now we're getting smarter. They insisted that we're nothing more than highly evolved animals without a soul or a purpose. In sociology, the teacher lectured on the absence of moral absolutes. Instead of setting a clear distinction about what is always right and what is always wrong, the lectures defined morality from the viewpoint of a particular culture or people group.

I knew what the Bible said. I knew the description of the beginning of life in the first eleven chapters of Genesis: "In the beginning, God created the heaven and the earth." And I knew that the Bible defines what is right and wrong, and calls wrong "sin." According to God's Book, sin is transgression of the law, the Ten Commandments. When I discussed the textbook ideas in class, I was just parroting the things I had heard because I didn't want to agree with God. I didn't want to be forced to fall in line with all those "religious" ideas. Deep down, I knew these things were still true, but I chose to suppress the truth to pander to the way I wanted to think, so I could live the way I wanted to live. I was fighting against the God Who made me by writing off the time-tested facts in His Book.

The parable of the Prodigal Son in Luke 15 aptly described my lifestyle during those college days, especially the part about "riotous living." The young man in the story took his inheritance and recklessly wasted the money and his time. At this point, I hadn't been to church or even opened the Bible in several years. I was working, attending classes, going to parties, getting drunk, and womanizing. If someone had asked me three years earlier, when I was at Bible college in Birmingham, if I were capable of doing the things that I was now doing, I would have self-righteously told them, "You're crazy!" My conscience had been seared: dead and hard on the outside but still fleshy and soft on the inside, like a steak that was seared but was still pink in the middle. I was so used to avoiding God's reminders that it was easy to do things my way instead, and I seldom even called it "sin" any longer. I was dead and hard on the outside like that steak on the grill. But inside, deep inside, there was a part of me that knew the truth: I belonged to God and He was calling my name.

In the hangar that day as I received my small pox shot, I felt fairly positive about the way things were going in my life. Despite being distanced from God and His plans for me, I was content with the way my life was going, for the most part. While I waited in line, I went through my checklist of three major items that had been weighing heavily on me for months. Two out of three were already taken care of, with the third one well on its way.

The first thing was Ciarra's birth and her miraculous healing, and that item was checked off with a deep sense of gratitude. At six weeks, she was completely healthy with no sign of the dangerous tumors that had once been growing on her brain. We thanked God every time we saw our little girl smile.

The second thing I had mentally checked off the list was the parachute investigation. In my mind, and in the thoughts of most of us in the platoon, the two culprits were in custody awaiting their trial and subsequent sentencing. I believed it was only a matter of time for justice to be done, allowing the rest of the platoon to breathe more easily and get back to our normal routines. None of us had any idea that Rayvens would soon name the Marine harassing Dickens in the hangar that day as the primary suspect of the sabotage. This affair was in reality light years away from being over and done with. The investigation would take a turn that I would have never imagined, and as strange as it may sound, the conversation I had with the XO in his office about Jude and Hartman would be at the center. In four months, my world would be turned upside down in a way that I didn't think possible.

The third item was the pending deployment, which was now underway. The months of waiting were finally over, and now we could get down to business. I knew that the sooner we left, the sooner we would return. This item wasn't checked off as completed, but it was certainly in progress, and soon we would deploy to a land ravaged by war.

Chapter Nineteen

Hurricane in the Desert

Nothing, however small, however strange, occurs without His ordering, or without its particular fitness for its place in the working out of His purpose. – B. B. Warfield

9 FEBRUARY 2003   CAMP PEGASUS, KUWAIT

After a sixteen-hour plane ride from Cherry Point, North Carolina, we finally made it to Kuwait City, Kuwait. By the time we landed, the "funk" that had been developing in my system was in full force. Walking down the steep stairs to the tarmac, I could barely stand up. The world was spinning in my head from the shots we had gotten before deploying, the two open holes in the back of my mouth, and from a sinus infection I had picked up. The sun was shining bright enough to give me a headache on the two-hour transport bus ride out to our camp in the middle of the desert. The worst of the dizziness and infection lasted a week, but afterward, I was never sick again for the duration of my time deployed.

When we got off the bus, we found a tent city, an established camp that had been functional for two months. Large Bedouin-style tents served as chow hall, chapel, administrative offices, and the general's headquarters, which was a matrix of adjoining tents connected by canvas hallways. Huge generators, extremely loud, ran air conditioning and electricity for lights and computers. This camp was home to 750 Marines and sailors.

This established camp was not our destination, though; we carried our sea bags a half-mile away through desert sand to a newer camp named Pegasus. Concertina wire (razor wire) stacked three high surrounded the perimeter of the camp, which measured a quarter mile square. Only a handful of sleeping tents in the center of the site had been erected, so we helped set up a chow hall near the front and acquired some generators for air conditioning. Headquarters and administration tents were set up in the rear, and after two more weeks, we got a shower facility and took much-appreciated showers every other day. Just walking from one tent to another took a lot of energy, especially in combat boots, due to the extremely thick sand. It reminded me of the beaches in Florida, although there was not a drop of water anywhere in the Kuwaiti desert. We had to slog through the unending stretches of sand to make a home for the duration of our deployment.

During the day, there was nothing but sand, as far as the eye can see, in all directions. At night, though, I could see the gleaming fires of the oil refineries burning brightly many miles into the distance. This time of uncertainty was another classic example of the ageless "hurry up and wait" game that we tended to play quite a bit. We staged our forces, performed equipment readiness inspections, and PT'd as best we could out in the middle of the dry and extreme desert heat.

While I was deployed with my platoon in the Middle East, the direction of the investigation was dramatically changing. First of all, Connery was released due to a lack of evidence after being in custody for two months; all charges were dropped. Also, Rayvens admitted that Connery had nothing to do with the parachute sabotage; he had made up the whole thing to frame Connery. I had always believed Rayvens over Connery, and my instincts had been one hundred percent wrong.

In terms of family, I didn't receive mail from Mary for almost a month, so that first letter gave me a much-needed connection to my wife and children back in the States. I read her letter over and over again, relishing details from home. Thomas, Mary wrote, kept calling for his Daddy, asking her where I was. He kept telling his mother he wanted to play with me. Reading that story about Thomas broke my heart; I missed that little boy of mine something awful. A few weeks after I received the letter, Mary sent me a care package with some things that were worth their weight in gold: baby wipes. Since we couldn't get a shower every day, the wipes were great for cleaning up and getting rid of some of the grit and sand. Also, she sent me a wonderful reminder of herself: a small pillow she had made from patriotic red, white, and blue fabric sprayed with her perfume. The pillow was about the size of an index card, and I kept it in the zipper bag she mailed it in to preserve the fragrance as long as I could. Any time the strain of being separated from Mary started getting too hard for me to deal with, I would open the bag and take a deep breath of the sweet perfume to remind me of her.

After about three weeks, we began to get into our "battle rhythm." We had our tent city fairly well established at Camp Pegasus, and we even had hot meals at the chow hall at night. The U.S. government set up contracts with civilians to run our chow hall, laundry service, and port-a-johns. This group of indigenous civilians became known as Third Country Nationals (TCNs). We looked forward to having hot chow every evening for several reasons. First, we had modified our work schedules in order to accommodate the daily afternoon sandstorms. During the summers in Florida, we can count on an afternoon rain shower every day; and in the desert, we planned our lives around the daily sandstorms. But the February sandstorms weren't anything like the ones I would experience in the Kuwaiti desert in June and July. In the summer, the sandstorms were made almost unbearable because of the heat. It was like trying to breathe with a hairdryer blowing hot sand at 50-MPH directly in your face. Also, the summer sandstorms lasted a lot longer than the ones in February.

The second reason we looked forward to the hot chow every night was the quality of the food. Mary would confirm that I'm not a picky eater at all: just give me a bottle of hot sauce and some black pepper, and I'll eat anything. Even so, the general consensus was that the food was excellent. They cooked a lot of local cuisine with flavors and spices including curry, which I like. It's amazing how much a good hot meal will do for morale when it's the only hot food we got all day long. When you're totally detached from most modern niceties, the little things mean a lot. This luxury would be short-lived, though, expiring when the war started in late March.

And finally, I enjoyed the hot dinner meal because I would get to relax and talk to the other officers in the battalion about how their preparations were going. Every other night after chow time, in the relative cool of the desert evening, I would take a shower in the "field expedient contraption" they had set up. Before this deployment was over, I would end up setting a personal record of three weeks straight without a shower, a record that I'm proud to say still stands to this day.

During the day we kept our platoon busy with attending classes. I gave several on the political climate of that region of the world and educated the junior Marines about why we were there to begin with. I was surprised to find out how few Marines were familiar with the geography of the Middle

East. For example, very few knew more than one country that bordered Iraq, so the regional classes helped orient them. Another one of my classes was a history lesson on the Iran/Iraq War from 1980 to 1988, as well as the first Gulf War in 1991, when most of these Marines were less than ten years old. This background was helpful to them in understanding just who Saddam Hussein was and why we were there: to help save the Iraqi people from that merciless tyrant.

26 FEBRUARY 2003 CAMP PEGASUS, KUWAIT

We had been in the northern Kuwaiti desert getting ready for battle for three weeks when we got a wake-up call. After chow time one evening, the battalion headquarters directed all of the officers to remain in the chow hall for a Professional Military Education (PME), which is a class given by a fellow Marine on a given military topic. Back in the States, we would typically have an officer PME once per month on a Friday afternoon at the Officers' Club. For this PME, we waited until all of the TCNs cleared the chow hall tent because the content was classified. Much of the information that was passed to us in that PME is common knowledge these days, centering on terrorism and radical Islamic terror groups. Up to that point, though, it was the first time that I heard much of it. I appreciated getting a clearer perspective on the enemy we were about to face.

When the class concluded at about 2200, I headed to my tent to get ready to hit the rack. It wasn't my shower night and the staff NCOs were already bedding down. About thirty minutes later, I noticed that it was starting to get a little windy outside. This was unusual, because the sandstorms always came in the afternoons. In the evenings the weather was always clear and calm. Suddenly, out of nowhere, the wind increased in intensity in an exponential manner. It was as if someone had flipped the switch on a wind machine.

Staff Sergeant Jude jumped up. "I'm going to go outside and tighten the lines on the tent, sir," he said.

All of us inside the tent started to stow away as many things as we could, because the wind was beating violently on the canvas tent flaps. The force of the wind started easing the long steel stakes slowly up out of the ground. Suddenly, one flew out, and then another. I ordered everyone to put their Kevlar helmets on. Jude was working hard on one of the guide lines inside the tent, trying desperately to keep it from collapsing, but the gale outside was too strong.

I shouted to him over the clamor of the howling wind, "Staff Sergeant, you better put your helmet on. Stuff's flying all over the place!"

"Aye, aye, sir!" he yelled back.

He reached down, picked up his helmet, and put it on. Before he could even secure the chin strap, an eighteen-inch steel tent stake popped loose and flew across the dark tent and hit him on the portion of his Kevlar helmet just above his eyes. The impact made him see stars and black out.

Trying to keep our tent standing turned out to be a futile effort, and it collapsed in rather short order. The entrance had collapsed, so we got on our knees to crawl out from under the canvas to find shelter from the 75-MPH winds. We struggled to find one of the junior Marines' larger and sturdier tents, but even though the tent was only 50 feet from us and we knew exactly where it was, we had trouble finding it in the pitch-black darkness of the sandstorm. We were walking blind: I couldn't see twelve inches in front of my face. For several minutes we stumbled around until we found the tent and collapsed inside.

Finally, some of the other Marines in the battalion formed a windbreak with all of the rolling stock vehicles that we had in the motor pools. It was great thinking, especially in the chaos and confusion of it all. With the 75-MPH wind sandblasting us, and in complete darkness, they formed a perimeter around all of the tents with seven-ton trucks and tractor trailers. If it hadn't been for the windbreak, I doubt any of the other tents would have been left standing. And then, after a few hours sitting in the dark in the larger tent, we eventually managed to fall asleep.

Daylight revealed the full extent of the damage from the relentless sand. Only one-third of the tents were still standing, and almost every person in the battalion lost some piece of gear. We had several Marines who lost both sea bags and had nothing left, but the only thing I lost was my Isomat (foam sleeping mat). They would later tell us that we had experienced hurricane-force winds of well over 70 miles per hour, making it the worst sandstorm in that region for forty years. During the storm, some people, such as the female Marines who were smaller and lighter, were launched into the air. We had a handful of Marines who needed stitches and one with a broken arm, but these were only minor injuries. Given the magnitude of the storm, it was miraculous that no one was killed: God's protection at work.

The next morning Jude was still talking about his near escape with the tent stake. "Sir, if you hadn't told me to put that Kevlar on when you did, that tent stake would have killed me! Sir, you saved my life!"

Jude kept repeating that to everyone he saw. He couldn't get over the fact that only a split second had elapsed between putting on his helmet and being hit with the flying tent stake. After several earnest repetitions of his gratitude to me, I started getting somewhat uncomfortable. I genuinely felt that the Lord had prompted me to tell Jude to put on his helmet, and I wanted him to realize God had saved his life, not Michael Dietrich.

"That was the Providence of God, Staff Sergeant," I told him. "I didn't have anything at all to do with that."

We worked tirelessly to get the camp situated again, and in a few days, it was hardly noticeable that a hurricane-force sandstorm had ruthlessly slammed into our unsuspecting city of tents. When everything was squared away, I received word that our air delivery gear and equipment had arrived at the Kuwaiti port and would be transported to us shortly, all fifty tractor-trailer loads' worth. Over the next few days, container after container of equipment arrived, and my platoon broke each seal and confirmed the contents in accordance with our embarkation paperwork. This check-in process kept us busy for the next couple of weeks, and it was a welcome break in the action. How long we would be in our current location in Kuwait or when we would begin our push northward into Iraq was still unknown. It was comforting, though, to see the tools of our trade finally arrive so we could support ground forces with air-delivered supplies.

In the middle of this equipment check-in process, I received some exciting news from battalion headquarters. The battalion adjutant came to me and asked, "Did you hear that the 'captain select list' is going to be published tomorrow?"

"No, I didn't know that," I said. "That's exciting. I hope I made the list."

The captain select list is a file of names posted every year of eligible first lieutenants selected by the promotion board at Headquarters Marine Corps in Quantico to be promoted to the rank of captain. Every officer rank from captain on up goes through this official screening and selecting process for promotion. Even though I knew that I was planning to get out when I got back to the States, I still very much wanted to get promoted to captain. There is a significant difference in the amount of respect and responsibility given to a captain compared with that given to a first lieutenant.

With a first lieutenant, my current rank, I was still generally referred to as "lieutenant": not second or first lieutenant, just lieutenant. As a first lieutenant, though, I was much more experienced with over three years in the Corps, compared to a second lieutenant who might be fresh out of The Basic School with only six months of training. Nonetheless, we were typically grouped together; it's just the way things worked. Besides that, there was something highly appealing about seeing those double-tracked captain's bars on a uniform instead of the single silver bar of a first lieutenant. At a distance, the metals of the first lieutenant and the second lieutenant were impossible to distinguish, and both insignias were single bars, so it was difficult to tell them apart. As curious as I was, the following day I was too busy to link up with the adjutant to find out about the promotion list.

That evening, I was walking to the chow hall tent, and I ran into the battalion adjutant. "Congratulations, Dietrich. That's exciting. 'Captain Dietrich' has a nice ring to it."

Surprised, I said, "Oh, I hadn't heard. So I got selected?"

"I'm sorry," she said sheepishly. "I thought you already knew."

Later that evening I found out that my number was 288. Starting in a couple of months, they would begin promoting a designated number of first lieutenants to captain each month. All I had to do now was to wait for my number to come up, and then I would officially be a captain. Unfortunately for me, the Marine Corps would promote approximately twenty-five a month, so it was very likely that I would be out before my number came up. Still, I was glad to hear that my name was on the list.

Within a couple of days of finding out that I got selected to captain, I received news from battalion that Staff Sergeant Jude had been promoted to gunnery sergeant. With promotions in my platoon, I always gave the Marine the choice of selecting the person he wanted to do the honors in the promotion ceremony. Having the opportunity to promote one of my Marines was always a highlight for me. Looking back on my career, I would have to say that it's one of the things I enjoyed most about being a platoon commander.

I approached Jude and said, "It looks like we don't have any staff sergeants in the platoon any longer."

With a confused look on his face, Jude responded, "What do you mean, sir? Am I...am I going somewhere?"

"No, Gunny. You're getting promoted to gunnery sergeant. Congratulations!"

"You had me going, sir," he said with a grin.

"Take some time to think about it, and let me know who you want to promote you," I said.

He instantly replied, "I've already thought about it, and I want you to promote me, sir."

With senior enlisted promotions like this one from staff sergeant to gunnery sergeant, usually the battalion commander or the company commander conducted those ceremonies. So for Jude to ask me, just a platoon commander, to promote him to gunnery sergeant was quite an honor. He honestly believed that I had saved his life during the sandstorm, and saved his career when I covered for him with Hartman and the urinalysis. With everything we'd been through together, I counted it an honor to administer the oath of enlistment and pin the new insignia on Gunnery Sergeant Jude.

CHAPTER TWENTY

Bunker! Bunker! Bunker!

The Fall is simply and solely Disobedience—doing what you have been told not to do: and it results from Pride—from being too big for your boots, forgetting your place, thinking that you are God. – C.S. Lewis

7 MARCH 2003   CAMP LUZON, KUWAIT

W hen we had been in our same location in the Kuwaiti desert for about five weeks, I began to sense a shift in the atmosphere. There was a lot more action in and out of the battalion headquarters tent, and various platoons began to get dispatched more frequently on convoys. At this time I received word from the battalion operations officer that my platoon needed to get ready to move out.

"You're going to Camp Luzon," they told me, "where you're going to link up with First AD Platoon. They're already there and have the camp set up. Camp Luzon is located adjacent to an expeditionary airfield and you'll be able to coordinate air delivery missions with the wing effectively from there. We'll have your platoon's gear re-located starting tomorrow."

The wing referred to the air component of the Marine Corps. Since we airdropped supplies to ground combat units, air delivery platoons were intricately connected to the wing. First Air Delivery (AD) Platoon was my counterpart unit from Camp Pendleton in California. The Marine Corps has only three active-duty Air Delivery Platoons: First AD in California, Second AD in North Carolina, and Third AD in Okinawa. My platoon would be joining forces with First AD from California. Over the next several days, we transported all of our gear to our new camp to the north, south of the Iraqi and Kuwaiti border.

Camp Luzon was a small camp with essentially no amenities compared to the camp we had come from. Inside the camp perimeter were several large Bedouin-style tents for living quarters, some communication and radar equipment along with a small detachment of Marines to operate them, a few Navy corpsmen, and a bank of greatly beloved port-a-johns. No more curry-flavored rice out here; it was Meals Ready to Eat (MREs) three times per day.

These military rations have changed a lot from the canned goods of the Civil War and the C rations distributed in Korea. Today MREs come in a variety of entrées from spaghetti to beef teriyaki and have a shelf life of three years. We never knew which main dish we would get, because they come in assortments, but spaghetti was my favorite. To heat it, we put the spaghetti package inside the green plastic heating bag and added a little water, which would cause a chemical reaction that got the food boiling hot in three minutes. Desserts like cherry-blueberry cobbler were also included, as well as packets of instant coffee and creamer. Of course, I always used the little bottles of Tabasco sauce on my food: the spicier, the better.

Outside the camp, we used the ship containers with our air delivery gear and equipment to our advantage, forming a perimeter to protect the work area that we had established. For rigging lanes, we erected tall, open-ended canvas tents with roller conveyors on the deck. We also had some smaller tents with packing tables in them, so we could re-pack personnel parachutes and small cargo chutes. In case the situation called for working at night, we positioned floodlights and generators in our exterior perimeter work area. And then, on top of some strategically located containers, we set up machine gun positions, hardened with sand bags. We put these sand bags, protection from enemy gunfire, anywhere we needed extra security, even inside a HMMWV. Since we were outside the camp's perimeter, we were somewhat exposed, so hardening was necessary for proper security of our equipment and Marines. We established a 24/7 rotating guard duty for these fifty-caliber machine gun security positions. And with all that in place, we felt reasonably safe.

After we got to Camp Luzon, I learned that First AD had deployed only their Marines and none of their gear or equipment. Before they left the States, they had gotten word that my platoon had embarked all of our air delivery equipment, so they left all of theirs in the rear. As we were getting snapped in to our new home, I quickly realized that we might have a power struggle on our hands.

First AD's Platoon Commander was a newly promoted captain, and I was still a first lieutenant. I hadn't received any guidance at all from battalion about the chain of command with First AD, or about whether I needed to report to them or to my company commander and Battalion HQ. In addition to that, all of the equipment was mine. I met with the senior enlisted Marines in my platoon, and Gunnery Sergeant Elway suggested forming Air Delivery Company by joining our two platoons together. "That way, there's not any question about chain of command, and also, we can build some unit cohesion between our platoons. Back in the day, there used to be an Air Delivery Company."

I considered this idea and prayed about it, asking God to show me the right answer. But my pride still didn't want to defer to the authority of a guy who was barely senior to me and had far less air delivery experience. The Lord quickly and clearly answered my prayer, though, with a distinct impression that I needed to submit to his authority and that Elway's proposal was the right one. If you were to plot my spiritual condition on a graph, the line would be very low when I went in to the Marine Corps, and even when I first took over AD Platoon. In the desert I was reading a lot from the Psalms in my camouflaged Bible, and from the Daily Bread devotionals they gave us. Using these readings as well as many other techniques, God had been working on my resistant heart, beginning with the parachute incident back in 2002, so the line on my spiritual graph now would be considerably higher. Little by little, the Lord of All was coaching me and priming me, because He knew a big lesson was coming up and He wanted me ready. Here in the desert He was continuing the training, and eventually He would re-design me to be an effective Marine under the Lord's command.

Feeling that the suggestion was a good fit, I approached First AD's Platoon Commander. "Good afternoon, sir. I'd like for you to consider joining our two platoons together in order to form Air Delivery Company with you as the company commander, me as your XO, and Gunnery Sergeant Elway as the company first sergeant. That way there's not any confusion among the Marines about who's in charge and what their chain of command is. In addition to that, when we begin executing missions, there needs to be a clear chain of command on our end when communicating with the wing and other supported units."

Captain Kent considered the proposal for a moment and then replied, "I think that's a great idea, Lieutenant Dietrich, and I appreciate you being willing to do that. My platoon sergeant mentioned the same thing to me. I look forward to working with you."

Kent was a tall, quiet guy who kept mostly to himself. He knew about my experience working with pilots, with the air wing, and with air delivery operations; and he let me and the senior enlisted Marines establish operational procedures and conduct liaison with the wing. I made sure to keep Captain Kent thoroughly informed, and I asked for guidance when I thought it was appropriate. From the start, we formed a good working relationship. Captain Kent was humble enough to avoid lording his authority over me, and as a result, I came to respect him and appreciated his leadership style. God was clearly working here; without this level of cooperation, our joint venture could have been very disruptive and ineffective.

Inside our camp, there was a detachment of air defense Marines operating a high-powered, sophisticated radar system. Their mission was to detect any threats from the enemy by air, such as missiles or rockets, and to provide advance warning to the Marines and sailors on the ground. They would also communicate that information to their cohorts who would intercept and knock the missiles out of the sky. We had developed an advance-warning system with a loud siren that would sound in the event of a potential incoming air threat. I rehearsed it with the Marines in my platoon at least once per day. If we were inside the perimeter of the camp when the siren sounded, the protocol was to grab the pack containing our nuclear, biological, and chemical (NBC) gear and our gas mask and to double-time it into the bunker dug into the embankment of the inside perimeter wall. If we were outside the camp in our work area, we took shelter inside a container that we had hardened with sand bags inside and out.

One week before ground forces would cross into Iraq, things got quite eventful. We were no longer in training or preparation mode: this was the real deal. For the next four days, the siren blasted its warning signal between thirty and forty times per day as the radar detected an incoming enemy threat from the air. As soon as the first Marine heard the siren, he would shout, "Bunker! Bunker! Bunker!" and then the rest of us would echo the warning call as we grabbed our gear and ran for the bunker. As we all waited in the prone position in the bunker for the "all clear" signal (three short blasts on the siren), we watched and most importantly, listened. After doing this routine about ten times or so, we identified a pattern.

After we sprinted to the bunker with our NBC gear and gas masks, we would usually hear a loud and resounding mid-air explosion forty-five seconds later. This was the sound of our ground-to-air missiles intercepting the enemy's missiles. Sometimes, the sound of the explosion was off in the distance, and we could barely hear it. At other times, the blast sounded like it was directly overhead, and indeed it was. We found several missile fragments in our camp for the next several days, dark and sharp, varying in size from a few inches to the size of a saucer.

The first dozen times or so the sirens went off, it was exhilarating and definitely got my blood pumping. By the end of the fourth day, though, we considered it more of an inconvenience. Even with the sound of missile explosions directly above and remnants dropping from the sky into our camp, I can honestly say that I was never fearful. The thought that I might die there in northern Kuwait seven thousand miles away from home due to a missile attack never even occurred to me. The Lord had given me a confident assurance that I would be okay.

Chapter Twenty-One

Shots Fired from the Rear!

Who has a harder fight than he who is striving to overcome himself.
– Thomas à Kempis

19 MARCH 2003   CAMP LUZON, KUWAIT

O n 19 March 2003, U.S. forces officially crossed into Iraq. My battalion then re-located from northern Kuwait into southern Iraq, about twenty miles from my platoon's location. I remained with Air Delivery Company at Camp Luzon with all of our gear and equipment and near the airfield with the sortie of C-130s.

After a week had gone by, my unit at Camp Luzon lost all communications with my re-located battalion. We had both UHF and VHF encrypted radios, but neither of them was working. We repeatedly tried to re-establish our communication link to no avail. My first thought was that they had switched frequencies and we didn't know the new ones.

In the absence of communication with my battalion, I focused my efforts in coordinating potential air drop missions with the nearby air wing. Unfortunately, the air wing didn't have any communications or "comms" with my battalion, either. They were receiving direction from their air wing headquarters who were communicating with the ground forces. But I had had no contact at all with my battalion, and neither had the other surrounding air units. In the two weeks since the war had officially started, I was getting extremely frustrated. Just then, a HMMWV drove up to Camp Luzon with two Marines from my battalion sent to check on us. "Ooh Rah, Marines! It's good to see some familiar faces! How are things going?" I said.

114

"It's going all right, sir," one Marine said. "We've been busy conducting re-supply convoy missions. Here's a satellite phone that battalion directed me to give to you, sir. You can call them on their sat-phone from this one if your tactical radios aren't working. These sat-phones aren't all that secure, though, so you have to be careful about what you say on them. Oh, here are the new frequencies. We changed them out about a week ago. Please destroy this sheet of paper, sir, after you re-program your radios."

The comm Marines from battalion departed my camp, and I got busy re-programming my radios and testing out the new sat-phone they left me. With the new frequencies programmed in, I attempted a radio-check to regain comms with battalion. "*Task Force Pegasus*, this is *Oscar-two-Charlie*, radio check, over." For a few seconds I waited for a response, but I got nothing except the buzz of constant static. I attempted again with the same results. Even trying both the radios got me nowhere: I was unable to re-establish contact. I opened the box to the sat-phone and began reading the complicated manual that came with it. When I finished reading it several hours later, I was finally able to get it set up and ready to use. I attempted to place a call to battalion's sat-phone, and it took thirty minutes to enter the security and country codes and wait for the satellites to triangulate both of our locations. Finally, I heard a ring and then a voice on the other end.

"This is Major Davidson."

Major Davidson was the battalion operations officer and was exactly the person I needed to talk to. As we attempted to talk back and forth, there was a challenging five-second time-delay for the message to transmit from phone to satellite to phone.

"We're ready for a mission, sir, whenever you need us," I said.

"Roger that, Lieutenant Dietrich," he said, "If we don't contact you, then make sure to call and check in with us every few days."

"Aye, aye, sir," I said.

I ended the call encouraged that I was able to finally talk to someone with battalion. However, I knew that it wasn't good news at all that even battalion hadn't heard from the unit that I was supposed to be supporting.

The communications problem was not resolved, and there was nothing I could do but wait. In the meantime, Jude and a few of my Marines had set out to manage some air drops with another unit, but there were delivery problems that required an officer's involvement. No one there wanted to head up the air drops, so in the end, Jude flew back to Luzon from Baghdad to request that I coordinate the missions to deliver needed supplies to Marines on the ground. With Captain Kent's approval, I flew back that night on a C-130 to the outskirts of Baghdad and traveled with Jude and Middleton with the logistics train for three weeks.

On the road with the logistics train, we were without tents or sleeping quarters of any kind. I asked Jude where he had been sleeping, since he had traveled with them before flying back to camp.

Jude answered, "Anywhere we can, sir. It's been tough getting more than a couple hours of sleep at a time with us being on the move so much. The most comfortable place I've found so far is on the hood of the HMMWV up by the windshield."

After checking out the HMMWV's that night, I discovered that all of the HMMWV hoods were already taken, so I slept sitting up in the passenger seat of a seven-ton truck. After a night of second-rate sleep, I met the captain the next morning in front of the operations center for the thirty-minute trip to the University of Baghdad and onto the campus where U.S. forces had their operations center. Although several of the brown brick buildings had been totally destroyed, the campus was relatively intact. The captain guided me through several open-ended tents until he finally located the tent he was looking for.

"Captain Peek, this is Lieutenant Dietrich from Air Delivery. He wanted to talk to you about coordinating some AD ops. Lieutenant Dietrich, I'll meet you at the HMMWV in a couple of hours. I have some things I've got to take care of."

As he made his exit, I sat down with Captain Peek to offer our services.

"Good to meet you, sir," I said. "I just flew in last night from Camp Luzon in the hopes of trying to coordinate some air delivery re-supply missions with you."

The pilot, Captain Peek, was easy to talk to. His tent was one of several very basic tents set up much like a refugee camp in the courtyard area of the University of Baghdad. Since Baghdad had just recently been secured, the tents were military-style shelters instead of the Bedouin tents we had at Camp Pegasus. They were crudely erected with only temporary amenities such as folding chairs and some field-expedient tables.

He looked at me with interest. "Air delivery re-supply? So what kind of items can you guys air deliver to us?"

"Sir, we can air deliver anything from a HMMWV on down to MREs and ammunition. We just have to get whatever it is that you need air delivered sent to us at Camp Luzon, so we can rig it up with parachutes, and then take it around the corner to the airfield and put it on a C-130."

"Do you have any truck tires? What I desperately need right now are truck tires. We're going through tires at a rapid rate," Captain Peek replied, alluding to the extensive tire loss due to improvised explosive devices (IEDs).

"Sir, it would be easy for me to rig up truck tires and then have them dropped wherever you want them," I explained. "The AD detachment with you would set up the drop zone, communicate with the pilot, and then de-rig it for you once it hit the deck. If you submit a request through your higher headquarters for an AD mission, they would have the tires sent to us at Camp Luzon, and then we would air deliver them to you."

We discussed a few more specifics about communications and the types of items that we could drop for them. Captain Peek was very interested in getting supplies air delivered, and I left very hopeful that we could be of assistance to his unit.

As Jude, Middleton, and I began our journey with the logistics train following directly in trace of the main combat element through Baghdad, the first thing that struck me was the number of Saddam's portrait on signs, posters, and buildings. From Baghdad all the way to Tikrit in northwest Iraq, his smiling face with its trademark big bushy mustache was plastered everywhere. Every light pole, spaced 100 meters apart in the median on the main road, held a two-foot by one-and-a-half foot metal sign bearing his image. As we drove by Hussein's huge statue, pulled down by a Marine Corps M88 tank retriever on 9 April 2003, I noticed brick buildings on both sides of the street with the entire facade covered by giant color portraits of him. This practice wasn't limited to Baghdad or the larger towns along the main road, either; all the small towns displayed his image everywhere as well. It was as if Saddam wanted to make it abundantly clear to his people that he was everywhere, and that he was watching, watching.

Middleton often drove the HMMWV, and we filled up the hours talking as we traveled through Iraq together through small towns with houses made of sun-dried brick covered with mud. Some of the villages had fewer than fifty people living there. Often we saw people with flocks of sheep, headed out to find grazing areas. Many villagers dressed in traditional robes and wore sandals, but some wore more Western clothing. We saw one man with a denim jacket over his robe and tennis shoes on his feet. There were very few vehicles of any kind in the small towns, so they looked quiet and peaceful from our vantage point driving by. However, we could hear gunfire in the distance.

On the northern outskirts of Baghdad, our convoy drove onto an abandoned complex of school buildings that included a museum and a mosque. We stopped for a couple of hours, so I got a chance to explore. Discarded military uniforms and various military paraphernalia were lying everywhere on the ground. I picked up a military shirt, an AK-47 ammunition pouch, an entrenching tool, and a black beret bearing the bronze insignia of the Iraqi Republican Guard. Apparently, the soldiers had stripped out of their uniforms and put on civilian robes to blend in with the locals undetected.

We departed again and headed north toward Tikrit, passing through several small villages, and soon we were in a relatively large town fifteen miles outside of Baghdad. All the small vehicles, bicycles, and people on foot in the middle of the road were slowing us down, so we headed off the main road and onto a side dirt road. In the convoy of about fifty vehicles, I was near the middle in a HMMWV with the four Marines from Second AD, with the HMMWV carrying First AD directly behind me. On the dirt road we were able to make about 15 miles per hour instead of the stop-and-go crawl we were doing on the main road. After five minutes, though, the convoy suddenly stopped. I assumed that the convoy commander was getting guidance about which route to take. We waited for almost an hour. Finally they gave the word to turn off the vehicles because of fuel level concerns and because some of the vehicles were starting to overheat. Jude and Middleton were both in the rear of the HMMWV with our supplies.

After ten minutes with the ignitions off, over my right shoulder, I heard close-range small arms fire.

"Pop. Pop, pop. Pop."

I instantly jumped out of the exposed HMMWV and shouted to my Marines, "Take cover! Take cover! Shots fired from the rear!" I ran around to the driver's side of the HMMWV in order to gain some cover between me and the location of the origin of the shots. With my M9 pistol drawn, a round in the chamber, and my weapon off "safe", I remember thinking, "What am I supposed to do with this little pea-shooter? It's only good for twenty-five meters. I need an M16 right about now!"

I quickly scanned the civilian Iraqi vehicles in front of me on the main road and the civilian Iraqis who were now scattering and frantically running for cover. I saw no one with a weapon, only hundreds of civilians wearing robes, trying to run for safety away from the crowd and from our convoy. All of the vehicles then began backing up, so I gave the order to the drivers to start the vehicles. First AD's HMMWV started right up, but mine did not. I ran over to the driver's side of my HMMWV and knelt down, with my weapon drawn, still watching the crowd. I asked, "What's wrong? Why won't it start?"

Sergeant Mendez replied, "I don't know, sir. It's completely dead. It won't start."

"Where are the slave cables?" I asked. "Slave cables" are jumper cables to civilians.

"I think they're in the other HMMWV."

Just then, another volley of shots fired from behind us, sounding even closer than before. The convoy began to move again, and vehicles started to go around my broken-down HMMWV as well as First AD's HMMWV behind me.

After a few minutes, Middleton, who had a way of doing what was needed to be done, found the slave cables. He hooked them up under the passenger's side front seat, and the HMMWV started immediately, to our great relief. We unhooked the cables, and I shouted, "Let's go! Let's go! Let's go!" With a dust cloud reaching thirty feet high, the last vehicle in the convoy passed us on the dirt road, and we pulled in right behind it.

Thankfully, no one was shot or killed in this incident, and we continued our march north toward Tikrit. I had never appreciated Middleton's resourcefulness the way I did when he found the slave cables just in the nick of time.

Day after day, we had the same experience with the Iraqi people as we drove through the small villages and towns. All the civilian inhabitants lined both sides of the streets cheering our convoy parade. They were smiling, clapping, and giving us the thumbs-up sign in approval of our presence in their country. It's regrettable that the media in the States did not report the grateful attitude we saw regularly displayed by the Iraqis. In all those little towns and villages, the Iraqi people were genuinely glad to see us.

On we went, driving for an hour or two, and then stopping for a few hours. We drove a lot at night under concealment of darkness, crossing both the Euphrates and Tigris Rivers in a total "blackout drive" on combat engineer bridges. One night, Jude was driving our HMMWV and Middleton was in another vehicle. As Jude drove up the bank on the opposite side of the Tigris River using only night vision goggles (NVGs), I said to him, "This is unreal! I didn't know a HMMWV could go up something so steep and not tip over!"

We were near the maximum angle the HMMWV was designed to handle: a 60-degree slope-climbing angle. The incline was so steep it felt as though we were climbing straight up at 90 degrees. At the base of the climb, the terrain was very muddy, but as we got farther up the bank, it became firm and grassy. I was impressed with the capability of the machine.

Jude just smiled and agreed. "This is awesome, sir!"

The landscape on our journey across the country of Iraq delivered some amazing, dramatic changes. In the southern region of the country, the desert stretched far and wide, with predictable colors of tan and brown. As we travelled north, though, the bland browns in the countryside slowly gave way to green, with colorful flowers and vegetation flourishing near the rivers and surrounding cities. Iraq is indeed a pretty country. Driving through the cradle of creation was somewhat of a sacred pilgrimage for me, and it was even more interesting to experience the journey with Marines from my platoon.

We finally made it to the outskirts of Tikrit and staged our convoy about five miles outside the city in a clearing off the main road. After dark, U.S. forces initiated air strikes on designated targets and the night sky lit up like fireworks all night long. When ground forces secured the airfield in Tikrit the next day, the logistics train and our convoy made camp on the interior of the airfield. We had been driving for four days straight with little sleep, so Middleton, Jude, and I were glad to be able to stop. I heard from headquarters that we weren't advancing any further north, so we would be in Tikrit for several days. After a full day at the secured airfield in Tikrit, I was looking forward to getting a halfway decent night's sleep on the hood of our HMMWV. As I climbed on the vehicle that night, looking up at the night sky, artillery and mortars were exploding in the distance near the edges of the vast airfield.

After fifteen seconds at the most, I was out cold. I'm not sure how long I had been asleep when I heard an intensely loud explosion a couple hundred meters away. I jolted off the hood, dropped to the dirt, and lay in the prone position, looking for the source of the explosion.

"What was that, Gunny?" I asked Jude.

"That's not friendly fire, is it, sir?" he said.

"No way! That has to be enemy mortar rounds or artillery."

The enemy forces lobbing fire on our position were too far away to see, but the explosions continued for an hour. Although most of the rounds landed in the distance, several landed within a hundred meters of our position. We were completely sleep-deprived at this point. The airfield was secured, with Marines patrolling the perimeter, and there was nothing further we could do. We couldn't see the enemy to engage him, so we just waited it out and finally fell asleep. Going through a night of enemy fire with Middleton and Jude definitely added a new level to our relationship.

The sun finally came up after that long night of firing, and the operations officer summoned my detachment to the main castle complex in the heart of Tikrit a few miles away. Saddam's complex, as well as several hometown castles, was located directly on the bank of the Tigris River. We drove up the steep winding access road to the main palace to inquire of our orders. A Marine approached me and said, "The operations officer is on the satellite phone with the colonel, so it'll be a little while."

While I waited, I wandered through Saddam's palace. Nearly everything inside was made of marble: marble floors, marble walls, and marble winding staircases. The ceilings were extremely high at thirty or forty feet, ornately decorated with Corinthian-style molding. Many of the rooms had beautifully painted ceilings which reminded me of the Sistine Chapel. After I toured the palace, I walked out onto a balcony overlooking the Tigris River. I could see a bridge, badly damaged in the air strikes, spanning the River and connecting Tikrit with the villages on the other side. With a panoramic view extending for miles in all directions, I looked down on these villages across the river and thought about Saddam. He had been living in the lap of luxury while his people were living like peasants in mud huts with dirt floors, all within a stone's throw from his marble shrine.

The operations officer finally approached me and said, "I need your detachment to airlift a water buffalo from the airfield to the village across the river. The locals go into town each day for food and water, but the bridge isn't safe to use, so we're going to provide them with clean, drinking water as a humanitarian relief effort."

"Yes, sir. How many days is this mission?" I replied.

"Three or four days," he said. "I'll let you know. You'll be out in the open without any security and all by yourself, so you need to be especially watchful. I'll send some military police in a security vehicle each night for your detachment."

A water buffalo is a bulk water storage container with a capacity of 400 gallons of potable drinking water. Its tank is on a trailer usually pulled by a military vehicle, but we airlifted this one to the opposite side of the river in a CH-53 helicopter. A herd of llamas from the village lazily watched us, and as soon as the tank was lowered safely to the ground, we distributed water to the locals. They brought their buckets, plastic jugs, and cups for us to fill, often traveling many miles on foot for the precious water. When the small thirsty Iraqi children gulped down their cupfuls of clean water and wiped their mouths with their sleeves, it was heartwarming to see firsthand the beneficial results from that simple mission.

For the next five days, as we distributed water to the local Iraqis, I had the opportunity to talk one-on-one with many of the Iraqi civilians. All of them were glad to see us; they weren't afraid or intimidated at all. Just like the civilians I had observed on my journey from Baghdad to Tikrit, these folks knew that we were "the good guys" and were there to help. I grew especially fond of a twelve-year-old Iraqi boy who spoke surprisingly good English. Every day, he would come to get water with a yellow plastic bucket and a big smile. He was very friendly; he would normally hang out with us for a couple of hours each day after getting his water, asking questions about American life. He taught me how to say my name in Arabic and even wrote "Michael Dietrich" in his language on a piece of cardboard from an MRE box, which I still have.

After we had been there a few days, I asked our young Iraqi friend, "So what do you think about Saddam?"

When I said that, he immediately began angrily kicking the dirt. As dust and dirt flew from the ground, the boy bent over and grabbed his sandal and started pounding the ground. He then heatedly shouted, "Saddam – no good. Bad. Saddam, bad!" There couldn't be a clearer illustration of the dictator's impact on the people of Iraq. When President Bush gave a speech about his capture on 14 December 2003, he spoke to the longsuffering people of Iraq, telling them they would not have to "fear the rule of Saddam Hussein ever again. All Iraqis who take the side of freedom have taken the winning side." Children like our little Iraqi friend would hopefully have a chance for a better life.

Back at Camp Luzon, I was glad to see Captain Kent and the rest of the Marines again, but the best thing of all was getting a shower. I hadn't bathed since I departed Camp Luzon three weeks previously, and my trousers could stand up all by themselves. I'm sure that I smelled bad, too, but I had gotten used to it and it didn't bother me at all.

After I had been back a week, I received word from battalion that we had a re-supply air delivery mission to support. We were tasked with air delivering MREs to support 2,000 Marines for three days. Twenty-five pallets of MREs were already rigged, staged, and ready to go; we quickly prepared twenty-five more for the C-130s to transport and deposit over designated drop zones. The following day, my unit transported fifty pallets of MREs, each containing a G-12 cargo parachute on top, to the adjacent airfield to be loaded. We loaded the rigged MREs into the C-130 and successfully air dropped them to the Air Delivery detachment on the ground.

Gunnery Sergeant Elway, my platoon sergeant, said in a matter of fact way, "You know we just made history, sir. This is the first Marine Corps air delivery mission conducted during combat since the Vietnam War."

That comment was all we needed after a long, productive day to make us feel we were doing something worthwhile. Morale was good, and the cohesion between First and Second AD was excellent as well. This mission was definitely a high point for the platoon, because we were serving fellow Marines exactly as we had trained to do, and making history at the same time.

Looking back on those days in Kuwait, and thinking about all the details of sabotage that came out after I returned to the States, I found it astonishing that Middleton was still in my platoon, traveling through Baghdad to Tikrit with me. Since at this point Rayvens had not yet named him as the main conspirator in the sabotage case, no charges had been made against Middleton and he was free to move around our camp. But according to Rayvens, it was Middleton's idea to "scare" me as an act of revenge. So here I was serving with Middleton seven thousand miles away, sleeping in the same tent. Despite the problems I had had with his poor judgment in Camp Lejeune, I actually grew closer to Middleton after everything we experienced together deep inside Iraq.

CHAPTER TWENTY-TWO

JAG

There is no neutral ground in the universe; every square inch, every split second, is claimed by God and counter-claimed by Satan. – C.S. Lewis

---

A few days after returning to Camp Luzon from the three-week trek to Baghdad and Tikrit, I looked from my tent to the entrance of the camp and saw two officers climb out of an Isuzu SUV. They were Marine Corps Judge Advocate General (JAG) officers assigned to the parachute case, representing the government by prosecuting Rayvens, who was still in pre-trial confinement at the Camp Lejeune brig.

They approached me and introduced themselves. "How are you doing, Lieutenant Dietrich. I'm Captain Ross, lead counsel in the parachute case, and this is Captain Bacon, who is assisting me. We need to talk to you alone for a few minutes."

"Nice to meet you, gentlemen," I said. "Yes, sir, we can meet in this tent over here." I led them over to the 15-foot Bedouin tent I shared with two other Marines. As soon as they came in and sat down, they dropped a bombshell: Rayvens had admitted to NCIS investigators that he had framed Connery, who had nothing at all to do with the case. I was so sure that Connery was lying and that he was in cahoots with Rayvens, but I couldn't have been more wrong.

"Connery has been released from the brig and is being assigned a different MOS, so he can transfer to a different unit," Captain Ross said.

"What about Rayvens' claim that Jude let Hartman go on leave to avoid a urinalysis? Tell me about that," Ross said.

This was old news. I was surprised they were bringing the urinalysis up; I hadn't thought about it much since my conversation with the XO in his office back on Camp Lejeune before we deployed.

I quickly replied, "Sir, Rayvens is trying to sling mud wherever he can. I talked to Jude and the XO about that, and it's not true. Jude told me that he let Hartman go on leave in order to deal with a family crisis."

"We have to get back first thing tomorrow morning to fly back out to Lejeune, but we're going to need to take one of your Marines back with us as a key witness in the case. Is Corporal Middleton here?" Ross asked.

"Yes, sir," I replied. "Will he be coming back?"

"Probably not, Lieutenant Dietrich."

At this point, I had not been given any information regarding Rayvens and his claim that Middleton was the mastermind behind the whole thing. Neither had I been advised of Rayvens' assertion that Middleton thought up the idea of framing Connery. The lawyers simply said that he was a witness and didn't mention any sordid details.

For the next few weeks, we were engaged in rigging air drop loads for the multiple requests that had started coming our way. After the first successful drop of MREs, word had gotten out to the ground units about our ability to air deliver supplies, and they started requesting our services. One of these missions was for a recon unit tasked with pursuing Iraqi forces attempting to smuggle weapons of mass destruction (WMD) across the border out of Iraq. We rigged up ammunition and nuclear, biological, and chemical (NBC) gear for them. I was briefed that military intelligence had information that mobile Iraqi units were transporting WMDs across hundreds of miles of unsecured borders out of Iraq and into neighboring countries. After I returned to the States, I was surprised to hear how controversial the WMD topic was. It seemed completely reasonable to me that WMDs were never found in Iraq: there were too many opportunities to mobilize the WMDs and transport them out of the country. I had personal knowledge of this because of the recon unit I was assigned to support. Their specific mission dealt with tracking these mobile Iraqi forces smuggling WMDs out of Iraq.

A month after the two Marine Corps JAG officers took Middleton back to the States, my unit was still at Camp Luzon, roughly twenty-five miles from the rest of my battalion. I soon received word from battalion that investigators were on the way back to my camp for follow-up interviews concerning the parachute case. One morning a dark gray SUV pulled up, and I immediately recognized Captain Ross as he stepped out of the vehicle. Ross brought with him an investigator from NCIS, a Marine named Corporal Strutt who was assigned to work with Navy personnel at NCIS, Camp Lejeune.

I met with Ross and Strutt in the same tent we had used for the first meeting, and Ross got right into the heart of the difficulty at hand.

"The parachute investigation," he said, "has led us in a different direction. We believe that there is a serious drug problem in your platoon. Middleton and Rayvens are both telling us about drug use being rampant inside Air Delivery Platoon."

I was amazed. "Sir, I don't even see how that's possible," I protested. "The entire battalion is drug tested so often that if there were Marines in the platoon doing drugs, they would pop positive. Since I've been platoon commander, we've never had a Marine test positive for drugs."

"Well, you'd be surprised about how creative Marines can get when it comes to taking a urinalysis," he said with a knowing look. "I've been doing this for a while, and I could tell you some things that would make your head spin. I've got a fairly long list of Marines that we're going to need to interview, so it'll probably take a couple of days to get through them all."

They interviewed several Marines that day, and later that afternoon I noticed that both of them were frustrated. Ross and Strutt were certain that the men were holding back information. They approached me and Ross declared, "I know that they're lying to me. They've all gotten together, and they're protecting each other." He frowned, looking over his interview list. "We need to talk to Corporal Denzell next."

Strutt frowned, deep in thought. "We may catch a break here, sir. I've got an idea to try with Denzell."

As I walked away to have my platoon sergeant get Denzell for the interview, my blood began to boil. These were my Marines they were bashing. I had been through the best of times and certainly the worst of times over the last eight months with them. Since the parachute incident on 21 September 2002, I had grown protective, and I had worked hard to keep my platoon from splintering because of the sabotage and the resulting distrust within our ranks. Before these investigators showed up, morale was surprisingly high and things were finally starting to get back to normal. But these two seemed overconfident, as though they were by far the superior players in an intricate game of chess. For the moment, though, the men were winning,

126

and Ross and Strutt couldn't stomach a loss. What I couldn't stomach was their treatment of my Marines, regarding them as convicted felons. I was furious.

I tried to keep my composure as we squatted down outside the tent. About ten minutes later, I looked up and saw Strutt exit the tent, bending over to move the thick tent flaps out of his way.

He stooped down beside us with a smile on his face and said to Ross, "I got an admission from him, sir. It took some doing, but I got it."

While they congratulated themselves on their hard-hitting interrogation techniques, I walked away from the celebration and went back to my tent.

In the midst of all the interviewing and re-interviewing, I talked to Jude. "I don't know how all of this is going to shake out," I told him, "but if they talk to us again about the thing with Hartman, we need to tell the truth – the whole truth. I don't know what drug use has to do with any of this or with the parachute case, but we just need to come clean."

He humbly looked at me and apologized yet again. "I'm sorry, sir, for getting you in the middle of the situation with Hartman. I'll take full responsibility for it. It's all my fault. You didn't have anything to do with it."

During the second day of Ross' interrogations, they interviewed Jude. The investigators ordered the gunnery sergeant to take Jude's rounds from his side arm and to secure them in the ammo box. Jude stood there, looking down at the sand, defeated. Immediately after the interview, they walked into my tent and Ross sat down on an ammo box.

"Lieutenant Dietrich," Captain Ross said solemnly, "we officially need to interview you now. Before we start, though, I need to read your rights to you. It's just protocol. I'm not calling you a criminal or accusing you of anything. We have strong evidence to support the occurrence of illegal drug activity in your platoon. I'm not saying that you had anything to do with it, or that you even knew anything about it. However, in light of this new information, it makes Rayvens' accusation about Jude and Hartman relevant to our investigation."

Then he began reading me my rights. *You have the right to remain silent. Any statement you make may be used against you in a trial by court-martial. You have the right to consult with a lawyer...*

Although Ross was obviously trying to downplay the serious nature of his remarks, I felt a sense of dread wash over me. He kept on reading my rights from the little laminated card, but the words just seemed to bounce around in my head. My feet felt frozen to the floor of the tent, and I knew that whatever lay ahead would surely be a period of hardship like nothing I had ever faced.

After the Miranda warning had been read to me, Captain Ross went on with his explanation of the details of Hartman's urinalysis incident. While he was still speaking, I jumped in. "Sir, I do have some additional information I need to share with you."

I gave Ross the added details of the exchange I had with Jude in the parking lot. As the investigator talked with me, his demeanor softened. Rather than the insolent, brash manner he had displayed with the men, he seemed to regret having to call me out. Trying to avoid looking me in the eye, Ross explained that Rayvens' claim of drug use in the platoon was legitimate, even though it was not an official part of the sabotage investigation. At that point, I realized what I had not seen before: by withholding information about Jude and the urinalysis issue, I had delayed the inquiry. Even though it was not deliberate, my action prevented facts from coming out about drug use, facts that would have led them to Middleton, the alleged mastermind of the sabotage that day in North Carolina. The feeling of dread never left me, and as we concluded our conversation, I knew that I was in considerable trouble. Later that evening, Ross and Strutt departed our camp and traveled to my battalion headquarters in order to de-brief the XO on the situation.

As I lay on my cot that night, I dreaded facing the difficulties that I knew was coming the following day. I was certain that I would be talking to the XO face to face soon, but I didn't know how it would turn out. What would unfold the following morning was something from a nightmare.

CHAPTER TWENTY-THREE

Relieved of Command

Sometimes the clearest evidence that God has not deserted you is not that you are successfully past your trial but that you are still on your feet in the middle of it. – Dale Ralph Davis

30 MAY 2003   CAMP LUZON, KUWAIT

I t was mid-morning, and I was within the perimeter of the camp when I saw another SUV pull up. All the Marines in my platoon and in Captain Kent's were outside working out with weights that my platoon had brought with us. My heart began to race when the XO climbed out of the vehicle. To my surprise, Lieutenant Fontaine, BTO Company XO and my good friend, got out of the vehicle as well.

I looked intently at the XO as he surveyed the camp. Suddenly his eyes met mine and he walked with rapid, determined strides straight toward me. From the look on his face and the aggressiveness in his gait, I knew things did not bode well for me. When he got within ten feet of me, I stood at attention and waited for his arrival in order to render the proper greeting.

"Good morning, sir," I said. He walked up close and got right in my face.

Towering over my five-foot-eight-inch frame, he bent slightly forward and glared into my eyes. "Lieutenant Dietrich," he said grimly, "I am relieving you of your duties as platoon commander. Lieutenant Fontaine is now Air Delivery Platoon Commander. You have ten minutes to pack your stuff. You're coming with me."

My heart sank. This was worse than I thought it would be. "Aye, aye, sir," I replied, overcome with embarrassment.

As I walked to my tent, defeated, only a handful of Marines saw what had just happened because most of them were still lifting weights. I stepped inside and feverishly packed my gear into two sea bags. Sweat dripped from my chin as I crammed my belongings in the bags within the ten-minute directive. With that done, I exited the tent, trying not to think about being relieved of my duties, and made my way to the SUV where the XO waited. By now, though, the entire company of Air Delivery Marines was there to watch me walk over to the vehicle in shame. The XO opened the swinging door to the trunk and I threw in my sea bags.

"Sit in the back," he said coldly.

As we sped off to battalion headquarters, there was total silence. Not a single word was spoken during the forty-five minute drive. Now, I thought, I had officially hit rock bottom. I had never been more humiliated in all my life: I was relieved of my command in front of my Marines. In OCS, when a candidate got kicked out, he would pull his sea bags in disgrace across the grinder to headquarters, where he would wait to be picked up and driven away. We would all watch, secretly thankful the dishonor was not ours. The long slow walk to headquarters, with sea bags pulled along the formation surface, was called the "sea bag drag of shame." Now, to my deep embarrassment, my men were watching me do the very same thing.

When we pulled up to Camp Pegasus where my battalion was located, the vehicle came to a stop, and the XO finally spoke. "You are to have absolutely no contact with the Marines of Air Delivery Platoon. They'll be coming back to Camp Pegasus shortly, but I am ordering you to stay away from them. Do you understand that?" he asked, his voice full of anger. "You'll be going up to see the general for NJP. In the meantime, you're assigned to the S-3 Shop, and you'll be working for Major Davidson."

I stepped out of the vehicle, got my sea bags out of the back, and walked over to my new home for the next six weeks: a Bedouin tent with six other battalion staff officers. In an instant, my world had fallen apart. I went from being the top-ranked lieutenant in the battalion assigned to the platoon everyone coveted to being a disgraced lieutenant who was humiliated, ashamed, and isolated. My plunge from top rank to deep disgrace was swift and severe.

In the Old Testament, there are many stories about the children of Israel wandering away from the Lord time and time again. When they would start honoring idols made of stone, I often thought about how thickheaded and stupid they were. They would do exactly the opposite of what God wanted them to do, get into trouble, and then repent and cry out to the Lord to rescue them. Of course, being the loving and forgiving Father He was, He would pay attention to their frantic appeal, show unwarranted kindness, and bail them out. After a while, the cycle would repeat as they wandered away from Him yet again to give their attention and money and time to other "gods." How dim and brainless I thought they were. What was wrong with them? Would they never learn?

Sitting on my cot, with my sea bags on the floor and my self-respect in shreds, God told me, "You are just like the Israelites." And He was right. I saw that I am exactly like those thick-headed, stupid men who lived so many centuries before. My Heavenly Father wanted me to give Him my whole-hearted attention. He wanted me to know Him more completely, understand His way of doing things, and be the leader my family needed. Doing things God's way is a win-win partnership for us: He knows what is best and He knows how to keep us out of danger. Why is that so hard for humans to see? For most people, plummeting to the earth with a butchered parachute the way I did on 21 September 2002, would have done the trick. Freefalling from an aircraft with a reluctant reserve chute would have definitely been enough for most people to do things God's way from that point forward. And that frightening moment was not the only warning sign God had posted for me: the astonishing healing of my little girl's brain should have given me a heart so thankful that I would be overjoyed to turn things over to the One Who created the world. But that didn't change me. The parachute failure didn't change me. In God's unlimited wisdom He knew exactly what it would take to bring about the radical change I needed to make. He allowed this dispiriting, agonizing humiliation to show me my thick-headedness, my stupidity, and my willfulness.

The God that knows when every 1.3-ounce sparrow falls also knew everything I was thinking and feeling. He knew that I had developed a habit of overestimating my own importance, an attitude He calls "a heart of pride;" and He couldn't get through to me when I was so focused on my performance, my skills, and my status. I was swollen with pride over my rank, my special platoon, my command, my physical abilities, and all my Marine Corps accomplishments. I liked knowing the men respected me, that I had earned the golden wings, that I was commander of the coveted Air Delivery Platoon. But God says that He is the One to be revered. He is the Perfect One Who deserves all my admiration. He says that smug self-importance is not only repulsive to Him but also destructive to me. I once heard a story of a wandering sheep who couldn't manage to stay with the flock. Every day, without fail, the shepherd had to leave the sheep and hike around to find the wayward animal, knowing the likely result for his adventurous sheep was disabling injury or even death. But the willful creature never learned. The frustrated shepherd began carrying the sheep on his shoulders to keep him out of trouble and save many hours spent searching the countryside. After many days of this restriction, of being so close to the shepherd, so near the sheep could hear every word his master spoke, the rebellious animal connected safety and security and love with his master. His affection for his shepherd increased a hundredfold, and he never wandered off from the flock into danger again. I could see myself in this story: the Good Shepherd was using this humiliation in the middle of the desert, seven thousand miles from home, to bring me back to Him. At long last, after everything that had happened, the Lord officially had my full attention. He had allowed my spirit to be broken so I could finally turn my ear to His voice.

I still have mixed emotions about that day; I can't really describe what I was feeling when I hit my new rock bottom. Before long, I was beating myself up over what I had done, which was lying to the XO. Although I never gave false information, I had concealed information, which I considered to be a lie. No doubt, it was wrong, and I needed to agree with God that lying is sin. But even though God had my attention, like the Israelites who went through the same cycle again and again, I didn't handle things Biblically at all. In hindsight, I know what I should have done: I should have humbly cried out to the Lord to forgive me and to claim the promises found in His Word, as John explains in I John 1:9: "If we confess our sins, He is faithful and just to forgive us our sins and to cleanse us from all unrighteousness." God was waiting for me to admit I was wrong, to agree that my sinful behavior was self-destructive. He wanted me to begin to see things from His perspective.

I should have found peace in Psalm 103:12, which explains that as far as the east is from the west, God has removed my sin from me. You can't get any farther than that. Also, I should have gone to the XO and asked for his forgiveness, admitting to him that I was wrong and telling him I was sorry. I should have done it that very day and not let the sun go down before I worked to restore our relationship (Ephesians 4:26-27).

But I didn't. I didn't cry out to God, agree with Him about my sinful conduct, accept His forgiveness, or restore my relationship with the XO.

Although I considered going to the XO, my thinking was so convoluted that I somehow convinced myself I deserved his contempt and reproach. Martin Luther, hero of the Christian faith, felt he warranted punishment to the degree that he would flagellate his back until it look like raw meat. Luther thought he had to suffer before the LORD would forgive him. One day, the LORD showed him Romans 1:17, which says, "the just shall live by faith." Luther realized this was a righteousness that God gave to people who didn't have righteousness on their own. It was all about God's gift rather than Luther's merit. Along those same lines, I felt as though I needed to suffer before I could be forgiven by anyone. Now, though, I know that this impression was a scam designed by the "accuser of the brethren." As Presbyterian preacher Steve Brown likes to say, the idea "smelled like smoke."

After being back at Camp Pegasus for a week, the rest of Air Delivery Platoon returned from Camp Luzon with Lieutenant Fontaine as their platoon commander. I was glad to see them again, but approaching them or talking with them was forbidden. What I was able to do, though, was talk with Fontaine. I hadn't told Mary about being relieved of my command during our weekly phone calls, because I didn't want her to worry about me, so Fontaine was my encouragement during this tortuous time. He wasn't ashamed to be seen with me, and he wasn't concerned about getting in trouble with the XO about being with me, either. We already had a lot in common, because we both had identical twin brothers, but during these weeks he became as close as my own brother. I remember that Fontaine would pray with me and read me uplifting Bible verses, such as Isaiah 40:31. In part, that verse says that people who look for the Lord and hope in Him will "renew their strength. They will soar on wings like eagles." The *King James Version* indicates that people who wait upon the LORD will run and not be weary, walk and not faint. God knew I needed a friend like Lieutenant Fontaine during that time of loneliness and despair. He helped me renew my strength.

Three weeks later, the battalion adjutant, Lieutenant Dwayne, informed me that I would be going to see the general in one week for my non-judicial punishment. She told me that Colonel Wood, the battalion commander, would accompany me and make a statement at the proceedings. In the midst of some very miserable days, this news was encouraging for several reasons. First, I simply wanted this whole ordeal to be over with; I wanted to get my punishment and then move on. Second, Colonel Wood had personally ranked me as the top lieutenant in the battalion on my performance evaluation, writing that I was among the most "exceptionally qualified" Marine officers that he had ever evaluated. I also knew that he had a special liking for me because I had given his parachute rigger father a tour around the paraloft.

Several days before I was scheduled to see the general, I found out that Colonel Wood's father had died. He would not be accompanying me to see the general after all because he would be flying out from Kuwait on emergency leave to attend the funeral. And in his place the Executive Officer, Colonel Simon, would be going with me to visit the general instead.

The night before meeting the general, I was summoned from my tent to the battalion operations center and directed to report to the XO. I walked slowly through the thick desert sand in the darkness of night, looking up at the sky. There wasn't a cloud in the heavens, and thousands of stars glittered across the shadowy expanse above me. God's design for the night sky was striking. During my short walk, I determined that I needed to ask for the XO's forgiveness before another day went by. I looked up into the star-studded heavens and earnestly prayed, "Lord, please help me" as I entered the operations center tent. It was another "flare prayer," but one that was heartfelt.

I spotted Colonel Simon, and walked over to him and said, "Good evening, sir. Lieutenant Dietrich reporting as ordered."

Surprisingly, he looked at me somewhat cordially. "Here's your fitness report that I need you to sign since you're going to see the general in the morning. Of course, it's an 'adverse report.'"

The colonel handed me the performance evaluation, which was processed ahead of schedule due to my ensuing NJP. This performance assessment was starkly different from the one before. In my last evaluation, my physical fitness test score on page 1 was perfect and my marks were so high that they required special justification comments by the colonel. In that previous review, I was ranked near the top of the Christmas tree formation of Marine Corps emblems on page 5. But on this latest evaluation, I was ranked at the bottom: dead last. Instead of being near the top of the tree, I was all the way at the base. From "exceptionally qualified" to "unsatisfactory": quite a downhill journey.

I quickly read through it, signed the back page and handed it to the colonel. Somehow I found the courage to ask, "Sir, I know that you're very busy right now, but I would appreciate a few minutes of your time later this evening."

He curtly replied, "You're right. I am busy. We'll see, Lieutenant Dietrich."

"Thank you, sir," I replied. "Good evening, sir."

I faced about and then walked back to my tent.

It was about 2130, and at that late hour, I wondered whether I would be able to talk to the XO at all. After two hours, I assumed that he decided not to see me due to feelings of anger or disappointment in my performance.

At that moment, a lance corporal walked into my tent and said, "The XO wants to see you, sir."

It was nearly midnight as I stepped outside my tent and headed in his direction. Colonel Simon was waiting outside the operations center. I walked up to him, and he kneeled down, gesturing for me to do the same.

With a measure of compassion in his voice, he asked, "What's on your mind, Dietrich?"

I cleared my throat. "Thank you for seeing me, sir. I just wanted you to know, sir, how sorry I am for what I have done. Not giving you the whole story about Jude and Hartman was terribly wrong, and there's no excuse for it. I know that I betrayed the trust that you had in me, and I'm sorry. I wanted to make sure that you knew that, sir."

"Dietrich, you're right. What you did was terribly wrong." The XO looked at me with concern. "But that doesn't make you a rotten person. Good people make bad choices sometimes. Now you're going to have to suffer the consequences of your choices. As bad as it seems right now, just remember that it will get better."

This was the first time Colonel Simon had spoken a decent word to me in weeks, and I was tempted to tell him why I had lied to him. I briefly thought of the merit of telling him about what I considered to be "extenuating circumstances," that Jude's family situation was deeply troubling him. Also, I considered Rayvens' drug claims to be completely unrelated to the investigation. For these reasons I told myself, "Apologize with no strings attached, no excuses. Take full responsibility for your actions."

As our conversation ended, I felt heartened by the XO's response to my apology. When I first got to his tent, I wasn't sure how he would react, and his manner was far more encouraging than I expected. And finally, I had apologized and asked his forgiveness for not giving him the whole story, which is what I should have done a long time ago.

CHAPTER TWENTY-FOUR

A Wrestling Match

The rougher the file—the less the rust. – William Tiptaft

20 JUNE 2003 CAMP PEGASUS, KUWAIT

The next morning I woke up at 0600, so nervous that I felt sick to my stomach. My meeting with the commanding general would mark yet another low point in my downward spiral. What would the result of the meeting be? What would become of my time in the Marine Corps? What was the worst that could happen?

The moment I had been dreading had finally come: my NJP proceedings with the commanding general (CG). Exiting my tent, I walked the half-mile through the heavy desert sand to the CG's tent, with no idea what would happen next.

The CG's aide stood outside the tent. "They're not quite ready for you yet," he told me. "Just stand by for a few minutes."

For ten minutes, I stood at parade rest outside the tent, growing more apprehensive by the moment. Finally, a Marine pushed his head through the tent flaps and said, "Okay. We're ready."

As I walked inside, the sergeant keeping guard at the entrance said, "Sir, I'm going to need to take your side arm while you're inside the tent, sir."

Another setback. Taking my weapon made me feel like a criminal, as though they didn't trust me enough to have a pistol and be in the same room with the CG. Without comment, I pulled my weapon from its holster, removed the magazine, and pulled the slide to the rear revealing the empty chamber. Then I marched inside and centered myself in front of the CG at his field expedient, lightweight desk. I stood at attention and said, "Good morning, sir. Lieutenant Dietrich reporting as ordered." Directly in front of me were the general and his legal officer, Lieutenant Colonel Reynolds, on his left. To my left, the XO sat silently in a folding chair. I stood there, nervous as I could be, but relieved to think that within the hour, I would know their decision.

The mood in the room was very solemn. Each officer waited with a serious look on his face; only the general appeared more business-as-usual, as though the outcome had already been determined. As I stood there, the legal officer then proceeded to read my rights to me. This was the second occasion someone had read my rights, and I didn't like it any better this time. *You have the right to remain silent. Any statement you make may be used against you in a trial by court-martial. You have the right to consult with a lawyer...*

While he was reading, I stood there gritting my teeth. Then the legal officer opened another folder and read from his script that I was being charged with making false official statements and obstructing an official government investigation. He brought out other documents containing supporting evidence, describing the meeting in the XO's office prior to deployment and the subsequent conversation with Captain Ross in Kuwait at Camp Luzon. He emphasized that my withholding information concerning the urinalysis that Jude allowed Hartman to evade hindered and slowed down an investigation that had not only national but also global media attention.

After the legal officer finished, the general looked at me and said, "Lieutenant Dietrich, do you have anything that you would like for me to consider before I decide on your punishment?"

Here was my one chance to help myself. "Yes, sir. I do."

"Proceed."

I remained at attention and took a deep breath. "Sir, I take full responsibility for my actions, and I know what I did was wrong. However, I do believe that there were extenuating circumstances in this instance. Sir, Lieutenant Colonel Simon directed me to ask Staff Sergeant Jude about the incident with Hartman going on emergency leave, and I did that. Jude told me that he allowed Hartman to go on leave to deal with a family emergency. This is what I reported back to the XO. When NCIS required my platoon to complete a questionnaire, I asked Staff Sergeant Jude again about it, and he gave me the same response. So up to that point, all I knew was that Jude had allowed Hartman to go on leave."

I could feel my knees shaking. In the formal setting of the NJP (non-judicial punishment), my head and eyes were straight to the front, even as I spoke, so I had no idea how any of the men were receiving my remarks. I just knew I needed to explain my reasons for not giving the whole story from the beginning. "Just prior to reporting to the XO's office, when I asked Staff Sergeant Jude for the third time, he finally told me that Hartman had sidestepped the urinalysis to avoid a positive on the drug test. Jude said he regretted his mistake, telling me that the pressure of some serious family troubles kept him from handling things as he should have. I didn't want to make things harder on Jude, and I did not see how avoiding a urinalysis connected to the parachute inquiry. Sir, I had no intention of obstructing the investigation by omitting any information at all, especially since I was one of the Marines who jumped with a sabotaged parachute."

Then the CG said, "Since Colonel Wood is on emergency leave, Lieutenant Colonel Simon will be afforded the opportunity to make a statement on his behalf. Colonel, do you have anything that you want to add?"

The XO then rose to his feet. "Yes, sir."

Before he began to speak, a sense of uneasiness washed over me. What kind of statement would he make? His remarks could sway the deliberations. Would he show a measure of compassion tempered with justice the way he had the night before, or would he treat me as he had during the previous month, and have no mercy at all? My mouth was dry and I swallowed nervously while I waited.

He read from a statement prepared in advance. "As an officer in the Marine Corps, Lieutenant Dietrich was given special trust and confidence, and he violated that trust in a most egregious manner."

My heart sank. This could not have been more humiliating. Over and over as he continued reading his statement, the XO used the word "egregious." Despite the concern he had shown me the night before, he clearly considered me to be low and disreputable, the very opposite of the picture of a United States Marine. The mercy that I was hoping he would display never came to light.

When the XO concluded his remarks, the CG looked straight at me and said evenly, "Lieutenant Dietrich, I believe you're a good Marine. No, you're not just a good Marine; you're a stellar Marine. Your fitness reports all confirm your excellent overall performance. However, your platoon is infected with a cancer, and you became infected with it as well. You became part of the problem and spread the cancer. Right here, right now, I'm going to stop it from spreading any further."

As harsh as I thought the XO's comments had been just a few minutes earlier, the general's remarks made them seem tame in comparison. In one breath, he said that I was a good officer; but then in the next, he compared me to a fatal disease. Could it get any worse? I stood there, feeling as though I'd been punched in the gut, waiting with apprehension for the general to give me my reprimand.

After what seemed like an hour, he began. "For your punishment, you will receive a reduction of half of your pay for three months. I'm going to suspend that since you're married with three young children. You will also be receiving an Official Letter of Reprimand that will be placed in your Officer's Qualification Record."

He then started to make some concluding remarks that indicated to me that the proceedings were nearly over.

I was amazed. Finally! It's over! It could have turned out a lot worse. But in that moment the CG's final remarks hit me full force. "A Board of Inquiry will convene to determine whether or not Lieutenant Dietrich is fit for duty to serve as an officer in the Marine Corps."

Then the CG said, "Before I conclude these proceedings, do you have any questions, Lieutenant Dietrich?"

"Yes, sir. I didn't understand the last statement the general made about a Board of Inquiry."

He replied, "Colonel Reynolds can answer those questions for you afterward. He's got some paperwork for you to sign as well. These proceedings are now concluded."

I faced about and exited the tent, and the sergeant returned my confiscated side arm. The general's legal officer followed me out of the tent and directed me to follow him to an adjacent series of large, connected air-conditioned tents. We found some folding chairs, and Lieutenant Colonel Reynolds explained the CG's comments about a Board of Inquiry (BOI). "A BOI is protocol when an officer goes through general-level NJP proceedings. The board will determine whether or not to retain you in the Marine Corps. Worst case, you could be administratively separated with an 'other than honorable' discharge. You do have another option, though."

My heart was hammering inside my chest. "What's my other option, sir?"

Reynolds looked at me with no expression in his eyes. "You can resign your commission. Your four-year contract is nearly up, and it's your intention to get out. The fact is that no one knows how long it will take for a BOI to convene, especially since it would be connected to the ongoing parachute investigation. It could take a very long time. If you resign your commission, you would simply transition out of the Marine Corps and avoid all of that. You will need to make a decision quickly about what you want to do and then sign one of these documents."

He selected a form from a sheaf of papers. "This one states you want to resign your commission."

Then he pulled out a different document and said, "This one indicates that you want to proceed with a BOI."

I replied, "How much time do I have to think about this, sir?"

"I've got to submit all of this today," Reynolds answered. "I can give you ten minutes." He stacked up his manila folders and walked out of the tent.

In terms of my career, things couldn't get any lower than this. Now, I had indeed hit the bottom of my deep pit of despair. I leaned over, put my elbows on my knees and stared at the floor. Fear suddenly fell over me like a heavy blanket. What in the world should I do? How could I possibly make a sane and logical decision about my future in only ten minutes? As I sat on that folding chair trying to force my brain to think rationally, my first inclination was to resign my commission. At least then I could try to move on with my life. I wanted the strain and anxiety and the pressure to be over.

The enormity of the decision weighed down on me, and I sat in that tent feverishly wrestling with a decision I had ten minutes to make. I was sick with uncertainty. I knew I couldn't figure it out, so I did the only thing I could think of: I closed my eyes and asked God for help. "Lord, I need You. This is so important and I don't know what to do. Father, please show me the right choice."

Just as I finished asking God to tell me what to do, I had a strong sense that I should not resign my commission. Even though my initial gut reaction was to do just that, my strong impression now was that God wanted me to choose the Board of Inquiry instead, depending on Him to get me through the process. In less than two minutes, the Lord had answered my question, and I felt almost lightheaded with relief. With His high-speed response, God had taken me from the total despair of an "other than honorable" discharge to a new sense of certainty that the BOI was the right alternative. My frantic appeal to the Creator of Heaven and Earth had been answered almost immediately, and I was cheered by the personal interest He had shown in such a fast response. God Himself was there with me in that canvas tent in the Kuwaiti desert, and He was still on my side today. Now I had no doubt about what I was going to do.

As the ten-minute limit approached, Lieutenant Colonel Reynolds returned and sat down beside me. "So what have you decided?"

With a confidence I had not felt ten minutes before, I replied, "Sir, I am not going to quit and resign my commission."

He looked at me, surprised. Clearly he had expected me to resign my commission, as most men in my position would have done. Without a word, he handed me the form that would set a BOI in motion.

For most people who decide to put God at the center of their lives, running every decision through Him, life after making that choice is not a cakewalk. There are times when things go well and you feel you're on the top of the world, but there are also times when life is hard and you feel worn out, spent, and alone. In the Bible, a man named Jacob had the remarkable experience of having a wrestling match with a Heavenly Being from sunset one evening till dawn. Some might insist that the fight was a dream, but during the wrestling match the Being put Jacob's thigh "out of joint," leaving him injured. A dream would not cause a residual physical problem. Clearly, it was a real fight. W. A. Criswell, whom Billy Graham once called the best preacher he had ever heard, put it this way: "What does that mean, wrestling? Some of you would know without my describing it. Wrestling, all night long with God. Hardest thing in the world, for a man to give up; that old Jacob's self somehow dies hard. That old, selfish, grasping you: I've got my plans, I've got my ambitions, I have my wants."[7]

In life, Jacob had made some very good decisions and some very poor ones. But like most human beings, he preferred doing things his way. Bible teacher Dr. Thomas L. Constable wrote, "God was bringing Jacob to the end of himself. He was leading him to a settled conviction that God was superior to him and that he must submit to God's leadership in his life."[8] Jacob would never be willing to do things God's way until he was able to see that God had a better plan.

This wrestling match was not a contest of mere physical strength, either: spiritual values were also in play. And in the same way that Jacob struggled with the Lord all during that long, long night, I had been wrestling with

Him for a long time as well: for years. Sitting in that canvas tent in the Kuwaiti desert, at the end of my rope, feeling totally helpless and full of fear, I sensed the Lord reach down and "touch the socket of my hip" as He had done to Jacob. In my case, though, it was my heart: God permanently changed my heart. In an odd way, I actually appreciate the on-going lower back pain resulting from the parachute incident. I thank God for it, crazy as it sounds, because it is a continuous, daily reminder of the discipline that brought me back to Him. I am not able to forget it, even if I wanted to. This relentless back pain reminds me of God's relentless love for me. All along, He had known exactly what it would take to make me willing to be overhauled by the Spirit of the Creator of all things, by the One True God. He knew I could never be ready to do things His way until I could see that He had a better plan. And He loved me enough to make that happen.

Over the next three weeks, I grew close to the Lord again and spent a lot of time talking with Him and reading His Word, believing that He would walk me through whatever came as a result of the Board of Inquiry. I knew He wouldn't drop me or abandon me, and I took courage from that as time wore on. In the Book of Psalms, David writes a lot about his enemies. Saul, a cantankerous king, was constantly on his trail, and David repeatedly fled for his life, feeling helpless. For example, in Psalm 57 David is hiding out in a cave, knowing that Saul's men are on the hunt. He compared his enemies to lions, calling them men whose teeth are spears and tongues are swords. Despite the danger that kept stalking David, he never lost his confidence in the One True God. Reading the verses David wrote so long ago encouraged me over and over again. God wanted me to have that same reliance on Him. In Psalm 46, David writes that God is our refuge and strength, an ever-present help in trouble. The same God Who walked David through those days of desperation would walk me through mine. I counted on it.

When the desert days were so hot and the sandstorms so frequent, we adjusted our work schedules, often sleeping in until 0800. To take care of business, we would then work well past midnight, when the temperatures dropped and the sandstorms were over. I got into the habit of taking walks in those cool night hours, with just the light from the moon shining down. Sometimes, I would walk and pray, talking to God about my life, Mary, the kids, the investigation, the uncertainties of my career with the Marine Corps. I was concerned about Mary's back, injured when she was picking Ciarra up from her crib, and I asked the Lord to heal my sweet, hard-working wife. Also, I was determined to be a better husband and father when I got home, and I asked my Heavenly Father to help me accomplish that goal. Then, at times, I would rehearse telling Mary about the mess I had gotten myself into, practicing different ways to break the news about the trouble I was facing. I didn't know exactly how to explain it.

Sometimes, Lieutenant Fontaine and I would talk together, since he was still willing to spend time with me even after everyone knew about my NJP. God knew I needed a friend! He would pray with me, prayers that were so encouraging during those anxious weeks before the Board of Inquiry. As we walked through the desert nights talking and praying, the Lord gave Fontaine a significant word for me to think about: *preserve*. My friend reminded me of that word many times in the desert and even back in Lejeune, waiting for the BOI. The word *preserve* reminded me of God's promise that He would see me through. Lieutenant Fontaine claimed in his prayers that the LORD would preserve me. I prayed that, too. I knew the whole situation would not magically vanish; I knew this Board of Inquiry was not going away. What it did mean was that God Himself would stick by me, all the way through. But more than that, even, my friend Fontaine believed that God would preserve my career. He felt certain that God was telling him I would not get dismissed from the Marine Corps with a negative report. Once again, I read the Psalms for comfort, knowing of David's desperation in those long ago days. The first few verses of Psalm 86 (*King James Version*) became my prayer.

Bow down thine ear, O LORD, hear me: for I am poor and needy. Preserve my soul; [. . .] O thou my God, save thy servant that trusteth in thee. Be merciful unto me, O LORD: for I cry unto thee daily. [. . .] For thou, Lord, art good, and ready to forgive; and plenteous in mercy unto all them that call upon thee.

CHAPTER TWENTY-FIVE

Heart of Gold

The terrible thing, the almost impossible thing, is to hand over your whole self—all your wishes and precautions—to Christ. But it is far easier than what we are all trying to do instead. – C.S. Lewis

10 JULY 2003   CAMP PEGASUS, KUWAIT

After being away from my family for five months, I was elated when the battalion received word that we would finally be going home. I could hardly wait to see my sweet wife and three children again. I wanted to hug my wife and squeeze my little ones and see how much they had grown. But as much as I looked forward to our reunion, there was something I wasn't looking forward to: I dreaded telling Mary about the disciplinary action I was facing with the Marine Corps. Since I had been back at Camp Pegasus, I was able to call her about once a week. But I didn't want to explain any of this to her over the phone, so I waited until I got home to break the news. I was ashamed and humiliated, and I loathed thinking that Mary might lose respect for me. Seeing a look of disapproval and shame come into her eyes was something I didn't think I could take, so I put it off as long as I could.

On 10 July 2003, we loaded our gear onto busses headed for the airport in Kuwait City. In the middle of the Kuwaiti desert the summer heat was nearly unbearable, even for a Florida native like me. The humidity was low, which was a good thing, but 130 degrees Fahrenheit is blazing hot no matter where you are from.

I'm not sure what the temperature was on the surface of the black tarmac as we stepped onto the runway, but it felt like 200 degrees with the air temperature registering 130. This time we boarded the military's version of a passenger airplane instead of the commercially contracted one we had before; no first class seating anywhere on this bird. So our return trip to the States was not nearly as pleasant as the seven-thousand-mile trip eastward had been.

Onboard the plane I settled into my cramped window seat near the skin of the aircraft, toward the front. We waited for thirty minutes with no air conditioning at all, and we were suffocatingly hot. Finally they told us they were having mechanical problems with the airplane and gave the order for everyone to remove their thick, desert-camouflaged blouses. But even without our blouses on, Marines started dropping like flies from heat exhaustion, so we filed off the plane and back onto the same air-conditioned busses that had brought us to the airport. On the bus, we enjoyed the relief of the cool air for forty-five minutes, until one of the air crew ran across the tarmac.

They had the plane running again. "Everyone needs to double-time it back on the plane, so it won't quit again. Once we get in the air, we'll be fine."

Oddly enough, the plane's mechanical problems didn't bother me one bit, and boarding a plane with questionable flight status seemed completely normal, given what we had experienced over the last five months in Kuwait and Iraq. We just wanted to get home, even if it meant that the engine was held together with duct tape and bailing wire. We hastily re-boarded the plane, had a successful take-off, and sure enough, everything was fine when we got in the air. Our half-way point this time was Shannon, Ireland, instead of Frankfurt, Germany, and landing in Ireland in the middle of the night meant I couldn't see the beautiful green landscapes I had heard so much about. Then, after another eight-hour leg in the air, we safely landed back home in the good old U.S. of A. at Cherry Point, North Carolina.

12 JULY 2003 CHERRY POINT, NORTH CAROLINA

This was to be a bittersweet reunion with Mary and the kids. On one hand, I was so excited to see her that I was about to burst out of my skin. But on the other hand, I was returning humiliated and full of shame. I had been relieved of my command, albeit after combat operations had been declared to be over, and my future was uncertain. I was depending on the Lord to see me through, as He had promised He would, but I struggled every morning to first hang on to the Spirit to keep me going and also to resist my human tendency to give up.

As we drove through Jacksonville, North Carolina, on our way to the base, we felt as though we were in a parade. Throughout the entire city, civilians were lined up on both sides of the streets cheering and holding up homemade banners as our busses drove through town toward Camp Lejeune. Some of the signs said, "Welcome Home, Heroes!" and some had "We're Proud of You" and "Semper Fi" painted on with bright colors. Many of them were family members of Marines, some still in Iraq. They held up small American flags, waving them as we went by. I was so proud to be a Marine and an American that day! Then, as we got closer to the base, a chain link fence was covered by white sheets with welcome home wishes from the families of our platoon. Mary had also made a beautiful sign for me that she hung on our house. What a reception it was for us.

On base, we headed straight for the armory to return our weapons. Since I had had a weapon by my side twenty-fours per day, every day for five months, I had trouble getting used to sleeping without it each night under the small brown pillow Mary had made for me to take to Kuwait.

Once our weapons were returned, we drove on to meet our families. After not seeing Mary for five months, I was strangely nervous about meeting her that day. The jumpiness I felt reminded me of our first dates, when I would be energized and jumpy all at the same time. Finally, our bus rolled to a stop, and I looked out the window trying to find her in the crowd of hundreds of civilians waiting at our battalion headquarters. But with so many people swarming around the bus I didn't spot her right away, so I went to retrieve my belongings from the storage compartments under the buss. I turned around, holding a sea bag in each hand, and there she was: twenty feet in front of me, wearing a pretty pink and white flower-print dress. As she tilted her head slightly to the right, she smiled, trembling, and raised her hands in front of her face, unable to stop the tears.

I walked over to her and dropped my sea bags at my feet.

Casting aside all Marine Corps rules about public displays of affection, I hugged her tightly and said, "I missed you so much. I love you with all my heart, Mary." She hugged me back and then, after a moment, leaned away to look at me. She took my left hand in hers and looked right in my eyes. "I think this belongs to you, Honey," she told me, slowly slipping my gold wedding band back on my finger. For a brief few moments, standing there with Mary, I had no thoughts of the parachute case or the trouble I was in or anything else negative at all.

146

After loading my gear into our minivan, I drove to our house on the base, which was just a few minutes down the road. Mary had asked a friend to watch our three children while she went to meet me, and I couldn't wait to see them again.

"So how is Ciarra doing? Is her head still okay?" I asked, glancing over at the smiling face of my wife and holding tightly to her hand.

Mary nodded. "She's fine, Dietrich. We've had some follow-up appointments, and there's not anything wrong with her. The reports from her six-month checkup all came back completely normal." Such wonderful news!

"What about the other kids? How are Thomas and Larissa?" Thomas was now four-and-a-half years old and Larissa was two-and-a-half.

She replied, "Oh, Dietrich, they've missed you so much! Thomas doesn't stop talking about his Daddy all day."

We pulled into the driveway, and I nearly ran to the front door. Mary stepped inside while I stood in the doorway right behind her.

With a big smile, she asked the kids, "Guess who's back and can't wait to see you?"

Then I stepped inside and saw Thomas and Larissa standing about fifteen feet away, by the fireplace. I reached out my arms and said, "It's me, Daddy. I'm back. Y'all come give me a hug!"

But Thomas and Larissa didn't move. They both stayed glued to the floor, with their chins down, looking over at me with big eyes. Then I realized they didn't remember who I was! Larissa was overcome with shyness, and ducked behind her older brother. Then I said again, with a big reassuring smile, "It's your Daddy! I'm back! You didn't forget me that quick, did you?"

Finally, Thomas walked slowly to me and hugged my neck, but Larissa remained standing quietly by the fireplace. To this day, I do think that she had probably forgotten who I was. She wasn't even two years old when I went overseas, so even though it crushed my feelings at the time to think she didn't know me, I can certainly understand it now.

That night, when the kids were settled down in bed, Mary and I finally had time to ourselves. I told her all the disturbing details about the trouble I was in and waited to see how she would react. I watched her face anxiously, and I will always remember my deep sense of relief when she held me tight and said, "Oh, Honey, why didn't you tell me earlier? It breaks my heart that you were going through all of that by yourself without anyone to talk to." She gave me all the support and encouragement I needed; I couldn't have asked for a better response. The more I told Mary about everything that happened in the desert connected to the parachute investigation, the more upset she became. "Why are they treating you like this? Did they forget that you almost died jumping with one of those cut parachutes?" Mary looked intently into my eyes and said, "Whatever happens, we'll go through it together. You're my husband, and I love you with all of my heart – for better or for worse, remember?"

Her words were an immense relief to me when comfort was my greatest need. Her reaction brought healing to my soul. Mary is the most compassionate person I have ever known: she has a heart of gold.

After some much-needed time off, my priority was to find out as much as I could, as quickly as I could, about the upcoming Board of Inquiry (BOI). Had none of this happened, I would be going on terminal leave and transitioning out of the Marine Corps in mid-September, just two months away. But now, nothing was clear. Everyday the unknown held me hostage: what would happen with the Board of Inquiry? What would my life be like after that day? My future was totally uncertain.

Chapter Twenty-Six

Big on Trust

If thou dost not stumble at this stone, the devil hath another at hand to throw in the way. He is not so unskillful a fowler as to go with one single shot into the field; and therefore expect him, as soon as he hath discharged one, and missed thee, to let fly at thee with a second. – William Gurnall

8 AUGUST 2003   CAMP LEJEUNE, NORTH CAROLINA

After I had been back in the States a month, I received word that the Board of Inquiry would convene in September, more quickly than I expected. I was hoping to transition back to civilian life in mid-September 2003, which was my original plan before any of this happened. That might be possible after all.

During this time, I was on a spiritual roller coaster. On some days, I was at a high point on the roller coaster track, feeling extremely confident that the Lord was going to work all this out. I felt the same certainty I had sensed in the desert when He had answered my frantic question about resigning my commission. I relied on Him, read words of encouragement in the Bible, and seemed to hear Him confirm His promise to see me through. As J.I. Packer put it, I had "a sense of God's presence stamped deep" on my soul. At other times though, the roller coaster went careening downward to the lowest point on the track, and I was in despair. I couldn't seem to make contact with God and the future seemed bleak and hopeless. On those days, instead of walking in confidence, I was wrapped up in desperation and felt like retreating.

Another reason my life was going up and down was the media attention, which had ramped up now that the platoon was back in the States. While we were deployed, reports of the sabotage had tapered off, but now reporters were revisiting the investigation, focusing their attention on the drug allegations against Middleton. Several articles centered on the narcotics charges, and then reported in the next sentence that an officer was relieved of command and received NJP. The implication was that the reprimanded officer was in some way connected to the drug case and the narcotics allegations. Although none of the reporters mentioned me by name, I knew exactly who they meant. And though I had no involvement in any narcotics use, some journalists insinuated that I was tied in to the drug investigation. At this point I unfortunately developed an extreme case of paranoia and became overly sensitive to people's attitudes, even when I was in town among civilians. The parachute investigation and the approaching BOI had become my whole life, and I assumed that everyone else, even total strangers, were dwelling on it as much as I was.

Mary and I had a weekend tradition of going out to eat, and we looked forward to resuming our date nights when I got back from Kuwait. The uncertainties surrounding my career, though, had increased the paranoia, and one night at a steak house, it kicked in. As we drove up and got out of our vehicle, a man in the parking lot started to stare at me. He was a civilian, over six feet tall, weighing about 200 pounds. After he turned around a few more times to stare, I had had enough. Angry, I walked straight up to him at the door of the restaurant to confront him and tell him off. As I got closer to the man, he motioned to someone behind me in the parking lot. Although I was certain the man had been staring at me, certain he was pointing me out, he had simply been waiting for a friend all along. Seeing that, my rage melted away and I realized I had hardly been breathing. My thoughts were so wrapped up in the investigation and the charges I was facing that I imagined every stranger wanted to pick a fight. I shook my head, disturbed by my instinctive response to the man at the steakhouse. Unfortunately, my sense of being watched increased to the point that I didn't want to go out in public unless I absolutely had to. I didn't even want to go to church because I knew that the majority of the folks there were Marines, and I didn't want to risk being recognized. I was obsessed with it, making my worries "fill the human eye with a false magnification," as William Wilberforce once observed. Everything in my present life appeared oversized to me, bigger than it really was, because anxiety over the upcoming BOI was tearing me apart.

In hindsight, I see that the Lord was showing me something about Satan's tricky schemes. Satan, the Enemy of God, loves isolating believers; for thousands of years, he has been very successful using this strategy. In fact, I strongly believe that one of the Enemy's most effective tools is to separate people who have asked Jesus Christ into their lives from other Christ-followers. The Bible explains that the devil is like a roaring lion, looking for people to devour. In nature documentaries, hungry lions on the hunt scan the desert plain for the gazelle that is off by himself, away from the herd. The lion will pick off the isolated gazelle every time. And it's the same way for humans. The devil, that prowling lion, wants to isolate people who try to live by the guidelines Jesus gave us. This particular tool of his works well; once he cuts a believer away from other people who depend on Jesus daily, the enemy plants thoughts of anxiety and fear. In Revelation 12, the Bible describes how the devil accuses Christ-followers day and night, bombarding their minds. But that same chapter in Revelation goes on to say that the believers overcame the accuser through Christ. The enemy did not win!

So as the days wore on, I continued my roller coaster ride, sensing the Lord's nearness one day and then feeling the next day as though He had moved far away. One week I would be confident and full of encouragement, and the next week despair would set in again. But in time, I slowly realized that God's promises held true whether I was encouraged or not, whether I was confident or not, whether I was in high spirits or not. And this truth stayed with me through the ordeal.

It was getting close to my Board of Inquiry, and the Marine Corps assigned Major White, a fairly new lawyer, to represent me. Right from the start, he didn't seem to like me very much. During our preparation time, I asked him about the process of resigning my commission. "So what would have happened if I had chosen to resign my commission? Would all this have simply gone away?"

He sighed, annoyed. "It doesn't work that way, Lieutenant. If you have pending legal issues, you can't just resign your commission to avoid them. If you had done that, they would have put your resignation request on hold until after the BOI was completed."

"Oh," I said, frowning. "That's not at all how Lieutenant Colonel Reynolds described it to me back in Kuwait. He said it was an either-or situation."

He quickly disagreed with that assessment and pulled some more forms from a folder. "He wouldn't have said that. That's simply not how it works, and he certainly knows that."

Major White's handling of my concerns surprised me, to say the least. How could I be represented by someone who didn't believe in me? With so much at stake, I decided to confront my lawyer then and there about his apparent lack of support for his client.

"Sir, I get the feeling that you don't like me and that you don't even want to represent me. Is that the situation, sir?"

Major White, taken aback by my bluntness, looked up from his paperwork. After a pause of several seconds, he answered, "What you did, Lieutenant...you violated trust in your chain of command. I'm big on trust, which is one of the main reasons I joined the Marine Corps: to trust each other with our lives. I don't think it gets much worse, what you did."

There it was, cold and clear. I could hardly believe that my lawyer, who was supposed to be on my side, had basically informed me that he considered me to be very low on his personal scale of integrity. At this news, my heart was about to pound out of my chest. I took a deep breath and tried to respond calmly. "Sir, I appreciate your being honest with me. That helps a lot. Could you explain how the process of requesting a different lawyer works?"

His eyes narrowed. "There's no process to it. All you have to do is tell me that you want a different lawyer, and then my boss will get you one. It's well within your rights to fire me if you want to. So is that what you're telling me? Do you want a different lawyer?"

I thought quickly. "No, sir, I simply wanted to know how the process works." In some odd way, I had the impression the major was hoping I would choose to fire him.

Then Major White added, "Well, just think about it, and let me know during our next meeting. We don't have a lot of time before the BOI, so if you do want a different lawyer, we need to do that quickly."

Just when I thought things would be somewhat predictable for a few weeks at least, I found myself in yet another situation where I didn't know what to do. I needed wisdom. I needed help. For the next several days, I asked the Lord to show me what to do about asking for new counsel, but I didn't seem to get a definitive answer. I consulted a few close officer friends, and every one of them recommended firing Major White after hearing that he had said, "I don't think it gets much worse, what you did."

When the time came for me to meet with my lawyer again, I still hadn't made a decision. I was leaning toward requesting a different lawyer, especially since there was so much riding on the outcome of the BOI. I drove to his office and parked in front of the red-brick legal building, and turned the ignition off. "Lord," I said, "please give me wisdom. I need Your help again. What should I do?" Very quietly, sitting there in the car, I felt the whisper of the Holy Spirit. *Trust me, Dietrich. Walk by faith in Me and not by what you can see. When I work all this out, I want you to know that it was My power at work and not your ability to fix it.* At last, an answer! God was reinforcing what He had told me before: if I depend on Him, He will work things out and demonstrate that He did it without my help. That was all I needed to hear. I stepped out of my car and walked down the sidewalk.

Major White and I sat across the desk from each other as we had the last time we met. Even though God had clearly answered my question just a minute ago, and even though I had believed Him, I found myself wondering how things would actually play out. I knew that I should keep White, as He had told me, but I was still too worried about the outcome to be at complete peace about it.

White looked at me unemotionally and didn't waste any time getting down to business. "Well, what's your decision, Lieutenant Dietrich? Do you want to proceed with a different lawyer?"

I quickly replied, "No, sir. I don't. I want to keep you as my lawyer."

The major raised his eyebrows, surprised. "Why? Why would you want to keep me as your lawyer, knowing how I feel about you?"

"Sir, I don't believe it's an accident that you were assigned to represent me. I believe that God has planned all this out. Just as you mentioned before when you said you were 'big on trust,' sir, I believe God is 'big on trust,' too, and this time He wants me to depend on Him to work things out."

When I said that, a very surprising thing happened. Major White's sarcasm and contempt began to melt away. By the end of the hour-long meeting, I could sense that he was genuinely on my side and wanted to help me. I walked down the sidewalk back to my car, praying: "Thank You, Lord. Please forgive me for doubting You."

After a few more meetings with Major White, the time had finally come for the Board of Inquiry. Nearly a year had passed since the parachute incident, and the inquiry was scheduled for the day after my thirtieth birthday. The range of possible outcomes from the BOI was far-reaching. In the worst case scenario, I could be kicked out of the Marine Corps and receive an "other than honorable discharge." In the best case scenario, at the other end of the spectrum, they could retain me in the Marine Corps and totally dismiss the case. It was, once again, a time to remember God's promise to get me through this and show me that His power made the difference, not mine.

CHAPTER TWENTY-SEVEN

Unbecoming an Officer

He will heal all the remnants of haughty and self-confident wisdom in us.
– François Fénelon

18 SEPTEMBER 2003   CAMP LEJEUNE, NORTH CAROLINA

After living in a nightmare of embarrassment and uncertainty for four months, I was finally going to get some resolution. Whether things would turn out good or bad, I didn't know, but at least the long, exhausting wait was coming to a close. Mary and I were looking forward to putting the inquiry behind us and getting on with our plans for the future. The day for the Board of Inquiry had come.

I walked into the small wood-paneled courtroom and sat down toward the front beside Major White. Nearby was the empty witness box, slightly elevated; about five pews for spectators filled the rest of the room. In front of me were the three Marines who would decide my fate, the "Board" in the Board of Inquiry. Presiding over the trio was a full-bird colonel, and serving on the board with him were two lieutenant colonels. (A colonel's insignia is an eagle, or "full bird," while the insignia of a lieutenant colonel, a lower rank, is a silver oak leaf.) These gentlemen, who weren't lawyers and had not been a part of the investigation, functioned rather like a small jury, although this was neither a trial nor a court-martial. Their task was to look at my track record and to determine whether I should be allowed to continue serving as an officer in the Marine Corps.

Sitting to my left was Captain O'Mara, a Marine acting as the prosecuting attorney. His task was to present me in the worst possible light and attempt to kick me out of the Marine Corps with the worst "characterization of service" possible. Typically, officer contracts end at the time specified on the contract, but the Marine Corps was considering ending my contract immediately with this BOI. The phrase "characterization of service" is a snapshot of the quality of military service, and could lead to two rulings: punitive discharges (resulting in either dishonorable discharge or bad-conduct discharge), which did not apply in my case; or administrative separation, resulting in either honorable discharge, general discharge, or other than honorable discharge. In this case, the administrative separation would warrant an "other than honorable" discharge. My lawyer's job, of course, was to prevent that from happening.

Captain O'Mara called two witnesses: Corporal Strutt, the NCIS investigator accompanying Captain Ross to Camp Luzon in Kuwait; and Colonel Simon, who previously was the XO. I was surprised that Corporal Strutt was called to testify, since his main involvement was in the narcotics case against Middleton. He didn't have much to do with the parachute investigation at all. After a few minutes of listening to the questions that O'Mara asked, I saw his strategy: trying to prove that I had full knowledge of drug activity within my platoon and had intentionally covered it up. None of this was true, and I sat there in amazement. His basis for this untrue allegation was that I had lied to the XO about Jude's letting Hartman avoid a urinalysis. He ignored the facts that I had not known that Jude allowed Hartman to avoid the test because of minor drug use until the third and last time I questioned Jude, long after Hartman had transferred out of my unit.

After the surprising testimony of Corporal Strutt, Captain O'Mara called the newly promoted full-bird, Colonel Simon, as his next witness. Since the colonel had been transferred to a base out of state to work with reservists, his testimony was given via teleconference. Once again, the colonel had a prepared statement from which he read. And once again, he didn't cut me any slack. Over and over, he used his favorite word: *egregious*. I had the same sick feeling I had with him in that tent back in Kuwait.

Next, Captain O'Mara directed me to take the stand. As I walked up to the front of the courtroom to the witness chair, I wasn't nervous at all; I had nothing to hide. At this point O'Mara's line of attack was clear and I knew that there wasn't one shred of evidence to support that claim.

"Isn't it true, Lieutenant Dietrich," he began confidently, "that you knew about the rampant drug use problem in Air Delivery Platoon while you were the platoon commander?"

I replied tersely, "No, sir. I did not. I had absolutely no knowledge of that at all."

The next line of questioning from Captain O'Mara revealed that he didn't know the answers to his questions. This surprised me, because I thought part of the lawyer creed was "ask only questions for which you already know the answers."

"How long, Lieutenant Dietrich, had you known about the situation with Jude letting Hartman go on emergency leave in order to avoid a urinalysis when Colonel Simon asked you about it?" he asked.

"Sir, I *didn't* know about it," I said. "When the XO directed me to ask Staff Sergeant Jude about it, I reported to him the information that I got from Jude, which was that it wasn't true. Jude finally admitted it to me only a few minutes before I was summoned to the XO's office on 4 February."

O'Mara frowned at this. "Are you telling me that you had absolutely no knowledge at all about that situation until the XO brought it up to you to ask Jude?"

I instantly replied, "Yes, sir. That's exactly what I'm telling you."

Then Captain O'Mara shifted gears. He flipped through some pages on his legal pad and stepped in front of the table. "One of the primary suspects in the parachute investigation is a member of your former platoon who was allegedly heavily involved in buying and distributing drugs." He paused to glance at his notes and then looked directly at me. "You knew about the drug activity in your platoon, and that's why you lied to your XO and to NCIS investigators. Isn't that true, Lieutenant Dietrich?"

I flushed with anger. "Sir, I jumped with one of the sabotaged parachutes and came within only two seconds of dying and leaving my wife a widow. My wife was six months pregnant with our third child at the time of the incident. These two Marines tried to kill me. Why in the world would I try to hinder the investigation and cover up evidence when I was the target of their sabotage? No one wants to see the truth come out in the parachute investigation more than I do. I'm certainly not trying to obstruct the investigation. That doesn't even make sense."

Captain O'Mara seemed stumped by my response, and soon after that, the prosecution rested their case. Major White asked me only a few more questions since O'Mara had inadvertently established in his line of questioning the main points my lawyer was planning to bring out. First, he wanted to demonstrate that I had no knowledge of drug use in the platoon, and secondly, that I knew nothing about Jude's covering for Hartman until 4 February. In less than two hours, the questioning was completed, and the Board asked me to leave the courtroom while they deliberated.

Time went by slowly while the Board discussed what they had heard. For two hours they deliberated, taking longer to deliberate than to hear the evidence. By this time, it was dark outside, just after 1800. Lieutenant Fontaine had come to the legal building to give me some much-needed support during the proceedings, and we sat together in a back room, praying. He thanked the Lord for preserving my life when I had jumped from the airplane with a sabotaged parachute, and he thanked the Lord for the way He was going to preserve me again in this Board of Inquiry. Fontaine kept repeating that word God had given him in the desert night, seven thousand miles away: *preserve.* I held on tight to the promise that whatever happened, God would preserve me, uphold me, keep me, and safeguard me.

I re-entered the courtroom to hear the recommendation they would be forwarding to the commanding general. I sat down in the same chair, next to Major White. My heart was racing.

The president of the board gave the ruling. "We have found that Lieutenant Dietrich has conducted himself in a manner that is unbecoming an officer of his grade and experience."

As soon as I heard that, I dropped my head and prepared for the worst. I knew what was coming next: they were going to recommend that the commanding general give me an "other than honorable" discharge from the Marine Corps.

Then he continued. "However, he has already been adequately punished for that conduct, and it's this board's recommendation to retain First Lieutenant Dietrich as an officer in the Marine Corps. If he chooses to transition out of the Marine Corps because of his approaching 'End of Active Service' date, we recommend that he receive full benefits and an honorable discharge."

In a span of thirty seconds, my emotions had swung from despair to elation. His first sentence was a death knell, but his second restored my rank. I went from possible "other than honorable" discharge to honorable discharge. I went from leaving the Marine Corps in disgrace to leaving on my own time line with my reputation intact. At long last, this nightmare was over.

When the proceedings had concluded and everyone had exited the courtroom, Major White filled me in on the deliberation of the Board. "Both of the lieutenant colonels wanted to just throw the whole thing out," he explained. "They couldn't believe you had been dragged through the mud like this, especially since you were one of the victims of the parachute sabotage. They looked at your fitness reports with your perfect PFT score and the 'Directed Comments' by your battalion commanders, and they didn't understand why your command treated you the way they did. The presiding colonel told them that they couldn't just throw it out, so that's why they reached the conclusions that they did. It all worked out well for you, Lieutenant Dietrich." He shook my hand. "I'm happy things turned out the way they did."

Two weeks later, I went on terminal leave, the Marine Corps equivalent of unused vacation time, and transitioned out of the Marine Corps, heading back to Florida with my wife and three children. Although I was very relieved to have this issue finally resolved, and to be leaving the Marine Corps with an honorable discharge, I left with a bad taste in my mouth. The disappointment regarding the end of my four-year career stayed with me. Many times, the last thing done is the one that is remembered, and my last Marine Corps experience was hardly a pleasant one.

After several years went by, though, I have noticed that my assessment of the situation has softened somewhat. Although the final days of my Marine Corps career were filled with anxiety and disillusionment, I can honestly say that I do not regret serving my country in the Marine Corps for those eventful four years. I love the Marine Corps and do not feel any bitterness toward anyone involved with the parachute incident. I will always be a United States Marine, and I will always have a deep sense of pride at serving in what General Douglas MacArthur called the finest "fighting organization in the world."

I've thought a lot about the series of events, reflecting on handling things differently. One question continues to come up: What would have happened if I could go back in time and tell the executive officer the whole truth? If I had not withheld the information about the urinalysis, I would not have gone through the agony of the BOI. But then, without the confrontation of my Board of Inquiry, would I have continued in my rut of estimating myself too highly? Would I have ever changed on my own, or would I have simply dug myself in deeper? The more highly I regarded myself, the less highly I regarded the Lord of All Creation. Despite the pain, the embarrassment, the bitterness of it all, I am glad I went through those dark days because I saw God's faithfulness and His forgiveness firsthand.

Chapter Twenty-Eight

Guilty?

He who cannot forgive others destroys the bridge over which he himself must cross. – George Herbert

7 APRIL 2004   CAMP LEJEUNE, NORTH CAROLINA

What was the final outcome for the Marines who allegedly schemed to sever the suspension lines and possibly send a jumper to his death? The three suspects were Connery, Rayvens, and Middleton. Connery, who was named by Rayvens as the one responsible for cutting the lines on 13 parachutes, steadfastly maintained he had not committed the act of sabotage. Rayvens, faced with the hair and palm print that placed him at the scene, admitted he was involved. Middleton, named by Rayvens as the mastermind who initially cooked up the idea, denied it all.

Connery was cleared and all charges against him were dropped. Rayvens had claimed Connery was used to run errands and distract attention while Rayvens cut the chutes in the paraloft storage locker, but this was never confirmed.

Rayvens, who cut the suspension lines on 13 parachutes, including mine, said he had agreed to Middleton's sabotage plan because he was angry about missing his girlfriend's boot camp graduation when he was restricted to base. "I was pretty mad at the outcome. I'd call it fuming," he told reporters from the *Jacksonville Daily News* on 3 April 2003. Rayvens contended that Middleton came up with the idea to slash the suspension lines and told Rayvens to do the cutting since Rayvens was "the fastest packer in the paraloft." According to the *Daily News* article, Rayvens opened 13 deployment bags, cut the suspension lines, and put them back. "I put the

160

parachute back in the deployment bag, (and) made a closing knot tie (and) then rerouted the static line around the outside (of the pack)." During the court-martial proceedings, he also admitted he knew that someone could have suffered severe injuries or even died, because reserve chutes have a 50% failure rate. Rayvens plea-bargained with the prosecution by agreeing to give key testimony in Middleton's court-martial. In exchange, Rayvens pleaded guilty to four counts of aggravated assault, nine counts of reckless endangerment, and one count of destruction of government property. The judge cut his rank to private and discharged him from the Marine Corps. He was sent to military prison and served one-third of a twenty-year sentence.

As for Middleton, he was also court-martialed. During the proceedings of April 2004, he continued to claim complete innocence in all charges of conspiracy, destruction of 13 parachutes, assault with a means likely to produce death or grievous bodily harm, reckless endangerment, obstruction of justice, and drug use. Rayvens testified against him, giving evidence for nearly three hours, explaining how Middleton conspired to commit the sabotage. Evidence also revealed that Middleton had called another Marine's cell phone at the drop zone just after Puller, Valez, and I had deployed our reserves; the timing certainly seemed suspicious. Although Rayvens repeatedly named Middleton as the mastermind behind the whole scheme, at the end of the day it came down to Rayvens' word against Middleton's. A jury of six Marines acquitted Middleton of all parachute-related charges but found him guilty of drug-related crimes involving marijuana and cocaine. His sentence was 39 months in prison, and he was discharged from the Marine Corps.

During his court martial, Rayvens' attorney showed video footage of his church, where Rayvens was preaching to a group of teens. I believe Rayvens, before he entered the Marine Corps, was a young man who depended on the Lord to order his life. A *Jacksonville Daily News* report chronicled Rayvens' response during the trial, quoting him as saying he "made the worst decision I could ever imagine." He went on, "Somewhere along the way, I went left where I should have gone right. I was wrong and I am sorry."

It's interesting to me that I have no bitter feelings against Rayvens whatsoever. In fact, if I saw him on the street today, I would shake his hand and hug his neck. He has been adequately punished for the bad decision he made; I can't imagine what it would be like to spend seven years in prison. Rayvens must have replayed that terrible choice over and over again in his mind. In many ways, my own Christian walk reminds me of his. For a long period of time, I did things my way without regard for God's plan. Because of bad decisions I have made, I could have easily done things exponentially worse than Rayvens' mistakes. My prayer is that he has returned to the Lord and that he has determined to spend time listening to his Creator every day. I hope Rayvens grabs every opportunity to tell everyone he meets how God redeemed his life. He could be a powerful example of God's relentless love, and people could be brought into the Kingdom through his story. I pray blessings from the Lord for him and his family.

What is the bottom line in all of this? Even after all the legal proceedings, I do not know the whole truth about the parachute incident. I've learned a myriad of things through this ordeal and one very important one is to never assume I know it all. Early on, for example, I was certain that Connery was involved in the sabotage, and I couldn't have been more wrong. Was Rayvens merely an accomplice in the plan? Did Middleton cook up the whole thing and then rope Rayvens in to cut the suspension lines? Who was at the center of the sabotage on that warm September day? I simply don't know. Middleton was acquitted by a jury of his peers of the parachute-related charges, and my sincere hope is that the jury got it right. And as strange as it may sound, I've come to peace with not knowing all of the sordid details. What's most important to me is how God walked with me through that valley and how He preserved me during those dark days of hopelessness. It's my prayer that I'm never in need of such a wake-up call again. I'm so grateful that He permanently changed my heart.

CHAPTER TWENTY-NINE

Re-wired

In the same way a Christian is not a man who never goes wrong, but a man is enabled to repent and pick himself up and begin over again after each stumble—because the Christ-life is inside him, repairing him all the time. – C.S. Lewis

4 OCTOBER 2003   FLORIDA

W hen we returned to Florida in 2003, we stayed with Mary's mother while our house was being built. One night, she turned on the television after supper and the three of us starting watching an episode of a new show called *NCIS*. The program opened with a Marine parachuting through the roof of a car. As the plot unfolded, sabotage was at the heart of the story: someone had poured sulfuric acid on his suspension lines. That got my attention.

My own sabotage incident was very fresh on my mind, and the Board of Inquiry was just a few weeks behind me. And as the program continued, NCIS investigators discovered drug use in the platoon. The similarities were striking, and I knew this story line was not a coincidence. As we watched the show, memories of my own experience were playing in my head: the painful drop with no canopy and a reluctant reserve, the extended investigation, drawn-out legal proceedings, the worry that whoever did it was still going through the daily routine with us in the platoon—it all came rushing back like a harsh wind on a cold day. I didn't want to dwell on it at all. I didn't want to remember the program I just watched. The parachute investigation and all the trouble I had gotten myself into was so embarrassing to me that I didn't even talk about it with Mary much at all. The enemy, that old accuser of the brethren, was again trying to drag paranoia back into the picture. And it worked, a little. He never gives up.

So why did the Lord allow all those experiences to happen to me and to my family? What did it all mean in the end? I believe God had several reasons in mind, and they all distill down to His endless, matchless love.

Struggles that Pushed Me to God

First of all, to put it bluntly, I needed a spanking. I was pushing my personal agenda hard, without regard for Mary, our kids, or anyone else. To reveal the damage this strategy was causing, the Lord disciplined me. He had tried to get my attention with the near-death parachute jump, but the arrogant condition of my heart kept me from seeing how serious God was. I was like a spoiled, immature little brat who didn't bother to appreciate the good things his dad had worked so hard to provide. My heavenly Father knew that the only thing that would show me, the only thing that would get through my hardheaded self-reliance, was hitting rock bottom. So He relieved me of my command. He didn't punish me to get even with me, or because His ego wouldn't stand for someone ignoring His rules. In very simple terms, my heavenly Father whipped my butt because He loves me. So why did He allow me to go through those events? The short answer is love.

In Hebrews 12, the writer explains that we should not resent correction from the Lord, because He disciplines only people He loves deeply. Verse 8 reveals that if we are without discipline from the Lord, then we are illegitimate offspring, without a father, and we are not really God's children at all. In light of this verse, then, I am particularly thankful that He loved me enough to correct me: His affection for me is strong. This segment of Hebrews paints a picture of a father who cherishes his much-loved son, welcoming the boy to his heart. So when the loving Heavenly Father disciplines me, I know I am unquestionably one of His cherished sons. Now that I have nine children of my own, I understand this principle much better than I once did.

Recently, I was reading Psalm 119, and the words resonated with me in a way they never had before. Verse 67, referring to living through tough circumstances, says, "Before I was afflicted I went astray: but now have I kept Thy word." Then in verse 71, the psalmist recognizes the benefit of his struggle, explaining, "It is good for me that I have been afflicted; that I might learn Thy statutes." In other words, the psalmist realized that the hardship triggered his change of heart. He had walked into tight spots, made some ruinous choices, and was chained to the unpleasant results. And then, in time, he saw that the harsh corrections were allowed by God, and they were actually a benefit rather than a curse. Through the disruptive and disturbing discipline, the psalmist started to see Who God was and how much he needed to know his Father.

These two verses could easily sum up the whole of my life. As traumatic as all of it was—the sabotage, the pride, the mistakes, the Board of Inquiry—I know that God was allowing those things to draw me back to Him. I was far from the Lord during those years; I had gone "astray," as the psalmist said. Oswald Chambers argued that this moving away from God was more than just carelessness; he called it "red-handed rebellion." Going through the sabotage and the subsequent investigation was at times frightening and demoralizing, but eventually all the negatives worked together for my benefit, because they drove me back to Jesus Christ. Now, years later, I can say that I am glad God took me through those dark days of speculating on who wanted to kill me and wondering how shattered my Marine Corps reputation would be. It wasn't easy when God began to take away the things I was so proud of. As concentration camp survivor Corrie ten Boom noticed, "It hurts when God has to PRY things out of our hand!" But once we humans understand our own inability to fix things, we are in the perfect position to see God's supernatural ability to fix everything. Those wrestling matches with shredded parachutes and nagging suspicions showed me clearly and powerfully just how weak I was, and just how much I needed a God Who was supernaturally strong.

In his collection of Puritan prayers, Arthur Bennett included this petition offered up to God by someone overshadowed by fear, humiliation, and defeat (xv).

> Let me learn by paradox
> that the way down is the way up,
> that to be low is to be high, [...]
> that to have nothing is to possess all [...].[9]

In the darkest place, the gloomy, sunless valley, the petitioner is crying out to God. He asks the Creator, in the middle of his downfall and his despair, to help him learn that all these struggles work together to lift him up, to take him higher. Even in his hopelessness, he is counting on God to show him how hardship leads to understanding. And He did. This is what happened to me.

<u>Re-wiring My Thinking</u>

An interesting thing happened as soon as we moved back to Florida from North Carolina: I developed an insatiable desire for reading. While that might not sound significant, it was for me. I was thirty years old, and I had never sat down to read a book for pleasure, not even once. In high school and in college I had to read a lot, but that was forced on me. I've always been more of the outdoor, athletic kind of guy. The thought of sitting inside to read, especially when the sun is shining outside, was a foreign concept. I would rather go fishing, play basketball, go for a run, or do anything other than have my nose in a book.

Although I had read the Bible occasionally, I wasn't motivated to find out what God was saying on those pages. There was no deep longing to discover what God wanted to tell me. But something changed me, and I was hungry with a hunger that was never satisfied. Instead of reading a chapter now and then, I was driven to do my best to find out what God wanted me to see in the lives of those men who walked the earth in ancient times. Over ten years later, I still can't get enough of His Word and books about His Word. I believe God gave me this craving to read the Bible for several reasons. First, He needed to re-wire my thinking, so I would set my mind on things above and not on earthly things. In other words, He wanted to broaden my perspective, to show me things from an eternal point of view. He wanted me to see that what was in my heart was what I cared about, and what I cared about was what I talked about. God wanted me to start thinking about Him, and what was in His book, so I would care about it, talk about it, and live it out every day. In Romans 12, Paul writes about being a "living sacrifice" and about not being "conformed to the image of this world." Then we're commanded to be "transformed."

So how do we do that? When I went to Officer Candidate School, I was simply Michael Dietrich. But during those weeks of intense training, I was transformed into a new man, a United States Marine Corps Officer. It wasn't easy. I had to change some habits and deny myself and leave my civilian ways behind. I had to learn the agenda of my Commanding Officer, and then do whatever he told me. Now, my Commanding Officer is my Heavenly Father.

He is a holy God, and as Francis Chan expresses it, a powerful one. "In heaven exists a Being who decides whether or not I take another breath."[10] If I'm smart, I will realize that this powerful Being knows much more than I do, and I will pay attention to Him and His Book.

Secondly, God took me through those difficulties to boost my understanding so I could use my spiritual gift. According to the Bible, the Father gives each believer at least one strong ability that makes him an asset to the Body of Christ, the group of people who have decided to take Jesus as their Lord and Savior. Then, when every Christ-follower uses his gift, such as helping people in difficult circumstances or leading a small group of people in Bible study, they do enormous good. For example, a person who has the spiritual gift of serving would help people by driving someone to the grocery store, mowing the grass for someone in the hospital, or cleaning out their gutters. First Peter 4:10 explains that followers of Jesus, having received a spiritual gift, should then use it as "stewards of the manifold grace of God". My gift is teaching. Naturally, God expects me to use this spiritual gift to explain to other believers what God's Holy Spirit has revealed to me. When I am planning to teach on a certain topic, I enjoy digging into the history of the Bible passage. I like getting out maps to show people where the story took place and describing what kind of people lived there. For some reason, God has given me a knack for taking a difficult topic and making it easier to understand, and people sometimes mention that to me after a class I've given. So I receive a blessing, too, as I teach.

Only recently have I understood that God intended me to start using the teaching ability He gave me with my wife and children within the four walls of my own house. In Ephesians 5, the Bible explains that the husband is the head of the wife as Jesus Christ is the head of the church. I am commanded to love my wife in the same way and to the same degree that Jesus loved the church and gave His life for it. Because of this important obligation, I will be held responsible for the way I love my wife and raise my children. First Timothy 5:8 says if someone does not provide for his own household, he has denied his faith in Jesus and is worse than someone who does not claim to believe. God has shown me that this teaching includes providing for my family's spiritual as well as physical needs, and so we are working on learning God's Word as a family at home.

From Arrogance to Concern

Another reason the Lord allowed me to walk through this hardship was to build in me a more sensitive heart so I could encourage people facing their own brand of adversity. Before I went through the difficulties I experienced in the Marine Corps, I had an arrogant heart of stone with little room left for compassion. If I saw someone suffering, especially as a result of their own wrong-doing, I had the attitude of "it serves them right." I'm glad to report that God has since replaced that stony arrogance with concern for people who are facing misfortune and tragedy. Second Corinthians 1 emphasizes that when God comforts us in our troubles, we can then use that experience to help other people in trouble. We have been on the receiving end of this comfort, and as a result, the Lord has given my wife and me a desire to bring to people the comfort that is so precious in dark days. Mary and I want to weep with people who are weeping, as Paul describes in Romans 12.

In February 2011, our family dealt with just that kind of tragedy. Mary and I had a miscarriage, an extremely difficult and emotional loss of our unborn child. We grieved over that little life, that precious little baby we never got to hold. Harvey, a good friend and brother in the Lord, gave me a book called *Heaven is for Real* by Todd Burpo. In this true story, a little boy goes to Heaven and sees a sister he had never met, because his mother had miscarried the little girl before the boy was born. Thinking back to the loss of our own little one, tears come to my eyes, and the comfort from Harvey's thoughtfulness and from the story was tremendous. Mary was also greatly encouraged when a woman in our homeschool group who had also lost a baby took the time to comfort Mary. Talking over the miscarriage and loss of a precious child with another mother was a priceless blessing for my wife. This friend sympathized with Mary's grief in a way that I never could have. And then, not long after Mary and I had struggled through our miscarriage, one of Mary's friends also lost an unborn child. Hoping to encourage her, we gave her a copy of *Heaven is for Real*, bringing full circle God's design for consoling His children. Our Heavenly Father is indeed the Source of every comfort.

Finding Balance

When I had been out of the Marine Corps about seven years, I developed an addiction. This was not a craving for drugs, gambling, or cigarettes, but an addiction nonetheless: I had become obsessed with running and cycling. When I had any free time, I would spend it on my bike or on a long run. There is nothing wrong with exercising; it is definitely important for physical well-being. But I had taken my interest in exercise to the extreme. For example, with cycling, I wasn't content with a thirty-minute ride. I had to ride for seventy-five or even a hundred miles. In the same way, running a few miles wasn't enough to satisfy my addiction. No, I had to run 26.2-mile marathons. Even though I was still reading God's Word, still being faithful to my church family, and still using my spiritual gift regularly, my unbalanced passion for exercise meant I was critically neglecting my family. C.S. Lewis recognized this over-the-top compulsion in *The Screwtape Letters*. This popular book, which was written as advice from one demon to another, details time-tested strategies for derailing believers. The demons, fiends such as Screwtape and Wormwood, recommend clever mind games and subtle suggestions to steer humans away from developing their relationships with the One True God, and in Letter 7, Screwtape writes, "All extremes, except extreme devotion to the Enemy [God], are to be encouraged."[11] In other words, the shrewd demon advised his underlings to drag humans down into any addictive behavior they could. Demons know that immersion in any one activity to the exclusion of everything else is dangerous, even beneficial activities such as maintaining a beautiful lawn, giving time to charities that help the homeless, or working out to keep fit. Mary knew my craving for exercise was out of whack, but when she brought up my compulsion, I would brush her off. I didn't want to listen to her concerns, much less discuss it and look for resolution.

Then one day, the Lord woke me up from my trance. I was on the phone that afternoon with my twin brother, and Daniel gave me a bolt from the blue. After fifteen years of marriage, Daniel was getting a divorce, and I could hardly believe it. He is one of the godliest men I know, and one of the best fathers I have ever met. I was heartbroken for my brother, my best friend. In that instant, on the phone with Daniel, the Lord showed me my mistake: my job didn't deserve my highest level of attention. Even my church should not be placed in such an elevated position; much less my running shoes or my bike. My first objective is to know the God Who made me, and He made it clear that the family He gave me was my second priority. God told me in no uncertain terms that focusing on running and cycling was channeling too much energy and interest away from Mary and my children. I felt as though the Lord had just splashed cold water on my face, waking me up from a dangerous, hypnotic stupor. Instead of being the husband and father and leader God had designed me to be, I was neglecting this family I loved so intensely. The time had come for me to take decisive action.

A No-brainer and a List

How do I go about re-scheduling my life? Before anything else, I asked God to help me. He prompted me to confess my mistake to Mary and ask her forgiveness. I told her I had been wrong to focus on my exercise regimen to the exclusion of my family, and she was kind enough to forgive me. Next, the specifics. My heavenly Father, faithful as He always is, gave me a list. The first thing I did was to stop running and riding: that was a no-brainer. Once that was done, I cut out things that were taking me away from my family, and this was more difficult. For example, although I loved singing in the choir, I felt God was telling me to stay home instead, because the weekly evening practices kept me from seeing my children at bedtime. When I was at church singing, all the responsibility for getting the children fed, bathed, in their pajamas and in the bed at a decent hour fell on Mary. The work we usually did together was all in her lap, at the time of day when she was most tired. In addition, I looked forward to this time, seeing them cleaned up and smelling sweet, growing drowsy as we prayed together before they fell asleep. So it was a lose-lose situation for our family. And even though music on Sunday morning is a valuable part of worship, sometimes there is a season of life that requires more time at home. Mary and I, with our growing family, were in just that season of life.

Also, God rearranged other parts of our schedule. For example, He showed me I needed to reduce the number of classes I was teaching at church, as much as I enjoyed them, because the preparation time took me away from my family too much. In addition, we took our oldest daughter out of gymnastics, because the three-hour practices three nights per week, plus competitions on the weekends, were tearing our family time apart. Clearly, all these interests are beneficial things: exercise, choir, teaching, gymnastics. We are in favor of them all. But when these good activities edge out the most important activities, the good things can become damaging things, and that's what was happening in our family.

After trimming the weekly schedule, Mary and I also instituted changes at home. For example, we started eating together every night as a family. Previously, Mary and I had supper at one table while the kids ate in the nook thirty feet away. To remedy this, we put the leaf back in the dining room table so we could all sit together. Before every meal, we hold hands and the kids take turns thanking Jesus for our blessings. I've made holding hands a big deal. We have a family joke they all laugh at: "The chain must not be broken!" In addition to eating together, another change we have made is adding family Bible reading to our nightly schedule. Every evening, we open the Bible and read several chapters. Then I ask questions, and the kids love seeing who can get the most correct answers. To help them learn where the books in the Bible are, we do Bible drills, and they race to get to the right page so they can shoot up their hands. Then before Christmas and Easter, we rotate story books about the birth and resurrection of Jesus, and each time the holidays roll around, they are a year older and better able to absorb the powerful truths of those events. The kids look forward to our time each evening and usually ask, "Can you read just one more chapter, Dad?"

God has prompted me to make several other changes as well. One is Family Game Night. First, we bought several board games like Monopoly, Life, and Apples to Apples to build up our stash, and now we all stay up late on Friday nights, two hours after the younger children's bedtime, and have a great time together. The kids look forward to it every week. I felt God was also especially interested in our television watching, so we cancelled the cable. We still have a television and watch DVDs, but we aren't absorbed in television watching like we used to be. God has been so patient with me through all this, and I'm very thankful that He is showing me, little by little, how to love Him and how to love other people, starting with my own family. I want to win the affections of my children, as John Piper writes, to help them understand the "mystery of the fatherhood of God."

As a result of these changes, our family has grown closer together. The kids know that I willingly gave up being a part of the choir, which I very much enjoyed, because I didn't want that weekly rehearsal to stand in the way of my relationship with the Lord and with them. They see that sacrifice and the reason behind it, and they feel loved by me and valued by me. They even treat each other better, too, which was an unexpected by-product of the changes we've instituted. And in addition, I've grown closer to my wife. During the months I focused on my exercise schedule, Mary knew things were out of balance and that the whole framework of our family was out of kilter. But my willingness to admit that I was wrong, and that I was neglecting her and our kids, was the first step in restoring that balance.

Mary's love language is quality time, so when she began to see me spending time with her and making time for our family, she was completely reassured that I loved her.

Little Things

In his book *Knowing God*, J. I. Packer explains what we are here for: "What were we made for? To know God. What aim should we have in life? To know God. What is the eternal life that Jesus gives? To know God. What is the best thing in life? To know God. What in humans gives God most pleasure? Knowledge of himself." The Maker of the Universe, the One True God, wants to have a personal relationship with every one of the human beings He created. Our Father Redeemer wants us to invite Him into every area of our lives, and He wants to fill us to overflowing with His Holy Spirit. From His exalted throne in Heaven, He cares even about the little things that we have trouble believing a mighty God would notice. When Jesus walked the dusty roads of Earth, He performed some spectacular miracles. He raised the dead, calmed a storm with just His voice, brought sight to the blind, made the crippled walk, and more. But he also dealt with some little things that didn't appear to be of great consequence. For example, He once healed a woman of a fever. In Matthew 8, the Bible describes Peter's mother-in-law, so sick from a scorching fever that she was unable to do anything but recline listlessly on her mat. Then Jesus, the One Who heals, reached over and touched her hand, and instantly her temperature returned to normal. This healing was clearly not minor to Peter or to his mother-in-law, but stacked up against some of the astonishing and amazing things Jesus did, healing a woman with a fever was certainly a little thing.

In the Old Testament, God used Elisha to perform a miracle concerning another little thing, relatively speaking. In II Kings 6, the Bible tells about a man who had borrowed an ax from a neighbor. As he was working down by the Jordan River, the ax head came off the handle, splashed into the river, and sank to the bottom. The woodcutter was very distressed not only from the loss of the tool, but also because he had borrowed the ax and now would have to replace it. Just then Elisha, known as "the man of God," threw a stick onto the water where the ax head dropped in, and instantly, the heavy piece of iron floated to the surface of the water for the man to retrieve. In other words, the same forceful God Who parted the Red Sea, so millions of Israelites could walk through on dry ground, was also concerned about someone whose name isn't even mentioned: a man who lost a borrowed tool one day down by the river. That's a profound truth. God cares deeply about the day-to-day struggles of each man and woman He created, whether the struggle involves an axhead or a day of Marine Corps discipline. This mind-boggling interest in the lives of human beings springs from a deep affection in the heart of God.

One little thing that had actually been a grave disappointment was the rank I received from the colonel just before I returned to the States. He had ranked me dead last in my performance review right before the Board of Inquiry. Seeing the X in the box next to the lowest Marine Corps emblem in the Christmas tree was a crushing embarrassment. But here is another "little thing" God did. When the BOI was over and I was leaving the Marine Corps, I received my last fitness report from Major Davidson. When I looked it over, I was elated. Major Davidson, who had been intimately aware of all the details of the parachute investigation and the BOI, ranked me in the top 5% of all first lieutenants he had ever evaluated. Even though he was a lower-ranking officer than the colonel, I valued his assessment highly since he knew everything I had been through. To go from the bottom back to the top was a gift from God's heart.

During my four years in the Marine Corps, I was very interested in another little thing as well. My promotion to captain, for example, never materialized. I was on the list, but by the time I transitioned out, they had not called my number. God knew that I very much wanted to be promoted to captain, but that never happened because of the trouble I faced after the parachute investigation. Because of the Board of Inquiry, my name was removed from the promotion list. But after I got out of the Marine Corps, I received letters in the mail every year for three years, stating that I was not selected for promotion to the rank of captain in the Inactive Ready Reserve. Each time I opened one of those notices, the wound re-opened and the pro-verbial cupful of salt was poured in.

After I left the Marine Corps, I returned to work for the same company in Florida. A co-worker happened to make a comment that may have seemed coincidental to him, but to me, it highlighted God's interest in my life. People at work knew that I was returning from the Marine Corps, but they didn't know anything at all about the trouble I had with the Board of Inquiry. One day, I was talking to one of the men in his office at the manu-facturing plant, and he gave me a nickname.

"You know what, Dietrich?" he said. "'Captain Dietrich' has a nice ring to it. I think I'm going to start calling you 'Captain Dietrich.'" Once he dubbed me "Captain Dietrich," it caught on like wildfire, and soon everyone at work was doing the same thing. For years, co-workers referred to me as "Captain," including people at the corporate office, and hardly anyone called me "Dietrich" for quite some time. Eventually I was transferred to a different plant where they simply call me by my first name; but when I occasionally run into people from the first plant and at the corporate office, they still call me "Captain." Is that just a coincidence? Just a random idea that popped into someone's head? I don't think so. Here is my Heavenly Father, who knew how much I wanted to earn the rank of captain, but He also knew that His plan for me was to leave the Marine Corps and resume my life in Florida. So, because God cares so much about even the little things we think about, He put the idea in the minds of my friends at work to call me "Captain." The Bible says that "even the things that seem accidental are really ordered by God" (Proverbs 16:33 *Amplified Bible*). God is so gracious: I'm continually amazed at the specific interest He takes in my life.

As you close this book, I urge you to remember one thing – God loves you so much. He has a very specific interest in your life, too. He wants desperately to have an intimate, love relationship with you. He knew you before He laid the foundations of the earth. He knit you together in your mother's womb. He is your Heavenly Father. Crawl into His arms and call Him "Daddy." Your Abba Father stands and waits with open arms; He loves you more than you will ever know!

How to Invite Jesus into Your Life

1. **Agree with God** that you have done things that are not right. Every human being has either thought, said, or done things that are unkind, untrue, or damaging. This could be as simple as telling a little white lie or as complex as stealing someone's car. God calls these wrong actions "sin." They separate us from God. The Bible explains that because of these sins, none of us can meet God's standard of perfection. Agreeing with God that this is true about your life is the first step.

2. **Accept what Jesus did for you.** When He died on the Roman cross so many years ago, He was paying for the wrong things you have done or said or thought. He never did anything wrong, but He loved you so much He wanted to pay for your sins. Jesus was your substitute. He paid for your sin with His death on the cross so you wouldn't have to be separated from God forever. Accepting His death as payment for your sins is step two.

3. **Ask Jesus to forgive you** of all your sin and come in to your life. He will do it. You don't need any impressive words or any religious lingo. Just ask Him the way you would talk with a friend. You could say something like, "Jesus, I need You in my life. Please forgive me of all my sins and come in to my life." You may not feel anything unusual when you invite Him in, but you can be sure He will come. He created you and He loves you intensely. Asking Jesus to forgive you is the third step.

4. **Find someone to help you** learn more about knowing Jesus personally. Just like any friendship, it takes time to get to know Him well. Jesus is looking forward to spending time with you! Reading His Book will help you find out more about Him and what He wants you to do. Talking with Him

on a regular basis will help build that friendship. And you will need a friend "with skin on" to help you. If you already know someone who loves Jesus and knows Him well, start there. If not, find a church where the people spend time talking about Him and singing about Him, and talk with someone who can help you get started.

5. Keep going. The enemy, Satan, does not want you to spend time with Jesus. He does not want you to read the Bible, talk with Jesus, or be around people who do. Be prepared to face some opposition. But Jesus loves you so much that He will help you through discouraging days. Getting to know other believers will help you, too, because they have all experienced the same struggle. They know that having Jesus in your life is the best thing that can ever happen to you. It's worth it! I can guarantee that, in Jesus' name.

ENDNOTES

[1] Russ A. Pritchard, *Raiders of the Civil War: Untold Stories of Action Behind the Lines* (Guilford, CT: Lyons Press, 2005), 46.

[2] *World War II: The Allied Counteroffensive, 1942-1945*, in *The New York Times Living History*, ed. David Brinkley (New York: Times Books, 2004), 26.

[3] Andrew Murray, *Abide in Christ: Thoughts on the Blessed Life of Fellowship with the Son of God* (London: James Nisbet, 1888), 93.

[4] François Fénelon, *Talking With God* (Brewster, Massachusetts: Paraclete Press, 1997), 63.

[5] Jonathan Edwards, *A Treatise Concerning Religious Affections* (Philadelphia: James Crissy, 1821), 270.

[6] Fénelon, *Talking With God*, 37.

[7] W. A. Criswell, "Emblems of Jacob's Pilgrimage", http://www.wac-riswell.com/sermons/1958/emblems-of-jacobs-pilgrimage/.

[8] Thomas L. Constable, "Notes on Genesis," 229.

[9] Arthur Bennett, *The Valley of Vision* (Carlisle, Pennsylvania: Banner of Truth Trust, 1975).

[10] Francis Chan, *Crazy Love* (Colorado Springs, CO: David C. Cook, 2008), 92.

[11] C. S. Lewis, *The Screwtape Letters* (New York: Bantam Books, 1982), 20.

CPSIA information can be obtained at www.ICGtesting.com
Printed in the USA
LVOW06s0605190215

427409LV00003B/3/P